MATTY MATHESON
A COOKBOOK

Matty Matheson

PHOTOGRAPHS BY
QUENTIN BACON AND PAT O'ROURKE

Abrams, New York

For Patricia and Macarthur

CONTENTS

INTRODUCTION

This cookbook is not about farms, gardens, sustainable seafood, or how much cocaine I did before or after service every night. It's about my memories of the food that I have eaten, cooked, and created. It's about time and place, like those moments during my childhood family outings at the beach, where we would eat oysters, mussels, and clams harvested from the waters surrounding a beautiful red-clay island. It's about how I looked up at Grampy shucking those oysters with his rusty pocketknife, then boiling and serving up the mussels and clams in his garage for me, my brothers, and my sister. This is a cookbook about these experiences. I will show you the food that has defined who I am.

I'm excited to share some of my favorite dishes, to tell you the stories behind my favorite foods. I'm going to be honest and real. I talk about almost burning down a restaurant or picking blackberries with my grandmother on the east coast of Canada. My hope is that we connect and that you get stoked about cooking and sharing good food. If this inspires you to go to a farm, a farmers' market, get on a boat, head into the woods, or walk with your toes in the sand through cold ocean water searching for oysters, then I've done my job.

Matty Matheson: A Cookbook is about my experiences with the dishes I've cooked and fucked up a thousand times to the ones I've loved, hated, and resented. This is that book. Starting on Prince Edward Island, where I found my love of seafood, to the woods of New Brunswick, where fiddlehead season was a highly anticipated event (even though I hated picking them), to the tough kitchens of Toronto, where I grew as a chef and as a person, this book is an honest recollection of the food that has molded me and made me the cook I am today.

Cooking at home and cooking in a restaurant are two very different things. At a restaurant, you have purveyors, farmers, and fisher folk a phone call away who can deliver pretty much any ingredient to your doorstep within forty-eight hours. You also have a brigade of cooks to help you with brining, pickling, smoking, grinding, cleaning, organizing, and everything else. At home it's just you, some family members, or your friends. Your son or daughter is your sous chef, your husband is a dishwasher, your grandparents are your guests.

The food in this book is for everyone to make at home, to feed family and friends. My family loves cooking. I'm sure if my grandfather wasn't a chef and restaurant owner, I wouldn't be a chef today. Spending the summers on PEI at the Blue Goose in Crapaud, DeSable, were the best summers a kid could have. I think of the garden in the back, the soda pop shop, and running around the dining room before the Goose opened. Playing hide-and-seek with my brothers, the club sandwiches, and turkey dinners. Eating bar clams and shucking oysters from the Northumberland Strait, boiling lobsters, mussels, and quahogs, and grilling steaks in the backyard of the restaurant. These were some of my fondest memories as a youth. I didn't even understand food but I knew I loved it.

I want people to make food, to cook food, to share food. Family traditions last for generations. If you don't have any, now is the time to start some. I love that anyone can turn a breakfast, lunch, or dinner into a ritual that could give a lifelong memory. The food is the foundation of the conversation. It will create a shared experience that will last. Even a poorly made meal could make for a lifetime of laughs, making fun of a sibling for overcooking his first apple pie or splitting mayonnaise he made for lobster rolls. It's about the cooking, learning, and sharing; these are my favorite times in the kitchen.

Often, you'll find whoever cooked the meal rarely eats at the table or has the smallest amount on their plate. I love watching the guests' faces at the table, seeing their first impression, eating the first taste of your love and efforts. Giggles, eye rolls, people looking like someone is under the table giving them some extra affection and attention. Those looks and feelings are what make the shopping, gathering, and cooking worth every effort. Food is one of the rare true experiences in this world. Food cannot lie: Either it tastes good or it doesn't. It's unapologetic that way. It's honest, and your job as a cook is to treat it that way. You are responsible for this animal or vegetable that a rancher or farmer spent his or her life cultivating. Don't fuck it up!

I wanted to share the joy that I find, no matter what I'm cooking. Whether that means making preserves, pickles, and salad dressings, shucking and cleaning shellfish properly, making terrines and pâtés, or cooking and basting meat. Hopefully this book generates the desire to set the table for years to come. The family table is so important to me now. Having my son, Macarthur, makes me think about what a meal means. I can't wait to start telling him my family stories (or most of them). Like the story of my dad stabbing a boning knife through his calf while cutting the ear off a cowhide. Or how my parents took the "gut truck" on their honeymoon when they were nineteen years old and went all the way to Moncton for a weekend of ZZ Top and Santana concerts.

Some of these recipes may seem difficult or may take a few days to prepare. Cooking takes real dedication. I was afraid to write this book, and now I'm afraid what people will think of these recipes or my history. I'm welcoming the world to my table. It's scary to think about that. There is an understanding that food can make you proud or embarrassed of where you come from. I wish I had the time to mill grain for bread every morning like my mother did. Or just have the energy to raise four kids! I really hope this book will take a little weight off the shoulders of mothers and fathers and give their families a new approach to cooking at home or on the beach.

Remember: It's important that we keep trying. You may first make underseasoned food or burnt food or undercooked food; it's more about the action and the time. Never give up. Keep cooking even if your piecrust looks like a torn-apart fence or if you overcooked and didn't rest your prime rib long enough. That's the point with food; it keeps pushing you to try again. Please try again and again and again. The one thing I want this book to do is to inspire everyone to cook. I just want you to cook something for yourself.

DeSable, Prince Edward Island, from Victoria Pier

PART I

Family

Edith and John Matheson

Nanny and Grampy in their absolutely stunning living room
in Woodstock, New Brunswick, 1967

Nanny cooking at the summer stove on the farm

MATHESON'S MEAT MARKET

The Matheson family has been on PEI since the late 1700s. Grampy was raised in Rose Valley on a homestead that is still in the Matheson family today. He was the ninth of ten siblings. He was a member of the Royal Canadian Mounted Police, also known as the Mounties. Grampy often went out on patrol with his dogs for thirty days or more at a time, surviving on what he could kill and carry on his dogsled. Nanny Edie was a Newfoundlander, born in Newfoundland. Like many from that time, Edie was very skilled at making food from the land, and the unique dishes of Newfoundland were carried forward by my dad in the form of salt-cod and Jiggs dinners.

Nanny and Grampy were both great cooks and used a lot of locally sourced meat, such as seal, caribou, ptarmigan, duck, sea trout, and whatever else they could get their hands on. Nanny's favorite wild game was porcupine! After a twenty-year career, Grampy retired from the RCMP at the age of thirty-nine. Grampy and Nanny then decided to move to Woodstock, New Brunswick, to buy a farm and start a slaughterhouse with a retail and wholesale meat store. Grampy added a commercial-size smoker to the operation, and they began smoking ham and bacon; homemade smoked meat was always in the cooler for delicious sandwiches. He also made his own sausages and a variety of charcuterie, like headcheese and blood pudding. They also had a massive garden, where they grew every vegetable imaginable, more than enough for their family and many of their neighbors.

Nanny and Grampy were very social people and would often have parties at the farm, where they would cook some of their specialties, like roast stuffed beef heart, beef tongue, sweetbreads, oxtail terrine, and potted meats, along with game such as deer, moose, bear, rabbit, duck, and goose. A lot of their friends had not experienced true Canadian food, so these events became legendary, and an invitation was highly sought after. They would start around eight in the evening and run until the next morning, with Nanny playing the piano and Grampy on his accordion, and others would bring fiddles and guitars, harmonicas, and the spoons.

Grampy was very entrepreneurial but would never admit it. In addition to owning the meat market, he was a skilled beekeeper. He typically had ten to fifteen active hives and sold a lot of honey. Nanny and Grampy had a sugar bush and made maple syrup for friends and family. They made cider from the apples of their orchard—five different types of apples grew there.

They made plum jam, cranberry sauce, blueberry jam, and blackberry jelly from the wild fruits on their farm. Not to mention the pickles—mustard, sweet mixed, chow-chow, dill, pickled beets. Fall was a very busy time. Nanny and Grampy loved to make these kinds of staples, and there was always enough to give away and to last until next fall. Nanny Matheson passed away when I was young, so we never really got to know her, but by all accounts, she was fun, smart, hardworking, and a great cook.

Eventually, Grampy sold Matheson's Meat Market with the intention of retiring on PEI. But he had to be busy, so he bought a restaurant that had been closed for five years. The Blue Goose in DeSable, down the road from Crapaud, a small village of three hundred people on the side of the Trans-Canada Highway, originally opened in 1947. Grampy made almost everything from scratch and used all local produce and meats. His breads and rolls were legendary, such that he opened a small bakery section so people could buy some to take home. Grampy's chowders were so popular that people would drive across the island to get them. The menu would change by season, and in the first few years he would close for three months during the winter. This caused hardship for some of his employees, so he started staying open year-round; even though he made no money in the off-season, the people who depended on the restaurant could work and make a living. That's the kind of guy he was.

When he passed away in 2005, so many people came by the house before and after to relay stories of how Grampy had fed anyone who needed it, that everyone who experienced a loss or sickness in their family would get a full-on turkey dinner with all the fixings dropped off. He cared about his community, and people knew it by his actions. That's probably why he was so successful as a police officer, a butcher, and a restaurant owner, not to mention a wonderful grandfather.

Top: Nanny with my dad aiming his BB gun at the camera
Bottom: Grampy (left) with some Arctic char in Yellowknife

Hot Butter, Cold Lobster

SERVES: 4
PREP TIME: 30 MINUTES

Salt water

4 (1½ to 2-pound/680 to 910 g) lobsters

Ice bath (water, salt, and 5 to 6 [10-pound/4.5 kg] bags of ice)

Unsalted butter

Growing up in the Maritimes was a beautiful thing. Living on any coast has massive benefits: the air, the beaches, the forests that surround them, the rivers that flow into the ice-cold salty water. What kid wouldn't love that landscape and terrain to run wild in?

There is nothing better than eating fresh lobster caught off the Northumberland Strait. The sweetness of this crustacean is pure mouth, heart, and mind joyfulness. When we would go to Prince Edward Island and my parents and Grampy would come back from the wharf with freshly boiled and chilled lobsters, we knew it was gonna be a long night of eating until we were sick of eating lobster!

I love cold lobster. I dislike hot lobster. I wanna hate it, but I still love lobster so much it's impossible to hate. I just feel that warm lobster takes away from the real experience of eating it.

In this recipe, you want that perfectly cooked lobster hit with warm melted butter. Cooking lobster is not that difficult, and you should always, always, always be careful to never, ever overcook it. You want the meat medium when you take it out of the boiling salted water. You don't want it to be translucent, and you don't want it to be overcooked and chewy. I find that boiling it for 8 minutes per pound is best. The ice bath is very important; it helps the meat release from the shell. Also, remember to salt your ice bath to really make sure that lobster is treated and chilled perfectly.

Set a large pot on your burner. If you have access to an outdoor propane burner, use that. If you don't have sea water for boiling, use ¼ cup (55 g) sea salt for each 1 (3.8 L) gallon water.

Bring the water to a boil and add the lobsters one at a time. Make sure you remove the rubber bands from the claws just before you put them in the pot. Usually, I flip the critters over and lower them headfirst into the water. Cover the pot; cook 8 minutes per pound, stirring about halfway through.

When done, drop the lobsters in the ice bath for 4 or 5 minutes. Timing is not critical here; if left longer, it will not harm the lobster.

Crack 'em open. I take the tail off and split it, and crack the claws just above the thumb. The claw legs have good meat, and a pair of scissors can be used to cut them open.

In a small saucepan, melt some butter and set aside when completely melted. Tear into your lobsta, dip, eat, and repeat until you can't do it anymore!

Chow-Chow

MAKES: 8 TO 10 ONE-PINT
(480 ML) JARS

PREP TIME: 3 HOURS PLUS
AN OVERNIGHT BRINE

4 quarts (4 L) green tomatoes, cut in half and sliced about ¼ inch (6 mm) thick

2 quarts (2 L) white onions, cut in half and sliced about ¼ inch (6 mm) thick

¾ cup (165 g) kosher salt

1 quart (480 ml) white vinegar

½ cup (110 g) mixed pickling spice

3 cups (660 g) brown sugar

This recipe is for what I consider a Maritime secret. I don't see this pickle much outside the territory, and it's a shame. These are great with any meat-and-potatoes type of dinner or as a garnish on burgers, hot dogs, and sausages. One-pint (480 ml) jars are the perfect size to keep or to give away to family and special friends. For me, homemade pickles are a trade item—I expect something good back!

—

In a large nonreactive container, put the tomatoes, onions, salt, and enough water to just cover. Let sit for 24 hours.

The next day, drain off all the liquid with a large sieve. Press on the mixture, but don't use so much pressure that you mush up the tomatoes. Put the drained tomatoes and onions in a 16-quart pot.

Add the vinegar, pickling spice in a spice ball, and sugar and simmer gently until desired tenderness. If you like your chow-chow soft, simmer for 20 minutes. For firmer chow-chow, check after 10 minutes.

Turn off the heat, and while the mixture is still hot, pour it into Mason jars using a funnel, cap them, and listen for the "doink" when the cap is pulled in by the cooling of the pickles. After about 15 minutes, test the tops with a gentle push to make sure they are sucked in. Don't worry: For any that aren't, you can refrigerate, or you can reheat and re-cap.

Store your pickles in a cool, dry, dark place; there's no need to refrigerate until opened.

Seafood Chowder

SERVES: 6 TO 8
PREP TIME: 1 HOUR

12 oysters

3 pounds (1.4 kg) littleneck clams, scrubbed

3 pounds (1.4 kg) bar clams, scrubbed

2 pounds (1 kg) mussels, scrubbed and debearded

2 pounds (1 kg) shrimp

4 large quahogs

Cornmeal

Kosher salt and freshly ground black pepper

½ cup (120 ml) good canola oil

4 onions, diced

4 stalks celery, diced

2 carrots, peeled and diced

2 leeks, cleaned and diced

2 cloves garlic, peeled and thinly sliced

2 tablespoons unsalted butter

2 cups (480 ml) good dry white wine

1 bouquet garni (a few sprigs of thyme, tarragon, and parsley wrapped in twine and tied to the pot handle so it's easy to pluck out of the chowder)

3 large Yukon gold potatoes, peeled and diced

4 cups (960 ml) heavy cream

Good olive oil for finishing

When Grampy used to take us clam digging, he would drive us down old dusty roads until we got to the crisp, salty air at his friend's beautiful beach on the south shore of PEI. My two brothers and I loved it so much. On the other hand, my sister hated it because she was a lot older and we tormented her so fucking much. We would throw sand, seaweed, mussels, and anything else we could get our hands on. My brothers and I were three little shits.

We would go, shovels and buckets in hand, as the tide went out into the Northumberland Strait. Grampy would tell us to look for air bubbles on the sand's surface. Then we would dig into the red sand, hoping to come up with bar clams, littlenecks, soft-shell clams, and the prized PEI mussel. We would walk farther out to the water's edge and find oysters and quahogs by feeling with our feet for little hard stones in the soft sand.

Grampy would sometimes just grab a few oysters and shuck them for us right then and there. Nothing beats that time in my life: looking up at Grampy in the hot sun, knee-deep in the ocean that's feeding you oysters. I was like a feral cat getting his first bowl of milk. I couldn't be stopped. Oysters are the best! Once in a while instead of an oyster, you would pull up a crab on your finger! As a child it was so scary—yet exhilarating—that this little monster clenched onto your finger, often causing blood to trickle down and drip into the low tide.

We would boil all the shellfish with salt water over propane burners in Grampy's driveway with the garage door open to let in the summer sun. Is there anything better? He would make this chowder the next day with whatever seafood was left over after we filled our bellies with mussels, clams, and oysters. He served it with hot butter and dinner rolls.

—

Clean the shellfish either by rinsing with cold water in buckets in the sink or leaving in a bucket with salted water and cornmeal in it overnight. Cornmeal makes the clams spit out all the sand in their bellies. Cleaning an oyster is easy: Place it on ice, scrub clean under cold tap water, then place in a tray under a wet towel until you shuck them for the chowder. Or just shuck a few to smash right then.

Shuck the oysters into a small bowl and try to keep as much of their liquor as possible. Place the bowl in the fridge with a wet paper towel over it.

Fill a large pot with water three-quarters high, add 4 tablespoons (68 g) salt, and bring to a boil.

Add your clams, cover the pot, and cook until they open, 5 to 10 minutes. Discard any that don't open. Scoop out opened clams with a spider into an ice bath. Do the same for the mussels. They should open almost instantly,

Recipe continues

within 30 seconds. If they don't open after 1 minute they are dead and should not be eaten. Scoop and place into an ice bath.

Turn off the boiling water and let it settle. It should look a little murky and kind of like watery milk. This is clam liquor. Once it has cooled a little, ladle from the top 4 cups (960 ml) of that beautiful oceanic liquor and set aside. Discard the rest.

Pick all the shellfish out of their shells; discard the shells. Place the meat in a bowl with a wet paper towel on top and put in the fridge with the oysters.

In another large heavy-bottomed pot over medium heat, pour the canola oil and add the onions, celery, carrots, leeks, and garlic. Cook until translucent, about 10 minutes—gently cooked-down mirepoix is one of my favorite things ever.

Once the veggies are cooked perfectly, add the butter and let it bubble and froth with all the mirepoix. Now add the wine, clam liquor, bouquet garni, and potatoes; cook 1 hour. Add the cream and the shellfish and cook 5 minutes, stirring continuously. Add and salt if needed.

Ladle into bowls and hit the chowder with a little drizzle of good olive oil and a few cranks of pepper.

Grilled Beef Tongue

—
SERVES: 8 TO 10
PREP TIME: 2 DAYS
—

½ cup (120 g) kosher salt

8 bay leaves

20 black peppercorns

2 bunches thyme

2 fresh beef tongues

2 tablespoons canola oil

3 onions, cut into large chunks

2 stalks celery, cut into large chunks

1 leek, cleaned and cut into large chunks

2 carrots, peeled and cut into large chunks

1 head garlic, peeled

3 tablespoons tomato paste

1 bottle (750 ml) dry red wine

1 bunch parsley

Kozlik's mustard, for serving

Tongue is one of those often mistreated dishes. Grandparents or parents back in the day either loved it or hated it. It comes from tougher times and was usually boiled and served right away, which would make for a dry meal. This is a recipe my Nanny and Grampy would make on the Green Road farm in New Brunswick that I've only heard about from my dad. And from what he has told me, Nanny Matheson was an amazing, knowledgeable, skilled cook and baker. She always cooked two tongues. While they were cooling, she would put them together in a 69 shape, wrap them tight with cheesecloth, press them, and chill them so they would make an evenly shaped loaf when unwrapped. She would then slice it and serve it as a cold cut; people had no idea what this delicious treat was, as it did not look like tongue.

I love beef tongue so much. Done right, it's better than pot roast. There are so many layers of hidden fat in the meat. The trick in this version is to peel the tongue while it's hot and place it back into the strained braising liquid to chill overnight and allow all the flavor and power to go back into the tongue. Let's all love tongue a little more and it will love us back tenfold.

—

We are going to make a brine for the tongues. This will give it a solid saltiness and keep the color nice and pink on the inside. We are going to end gray boiled tongues forever, right now! In a large 6-quart (5.7 L) pot, combine 5 cups (1.2 L) water, the salt, 4 bay leaves, the peppercorns, and a few sprigs of thyme. Bring to a boil, then let cool to room temperature. Add the tongues to the pot and cover the top with plastic wrap or place the lid on top. Let the mixture brine for 24 hours in the refrigerator.

In another large pot over medium-high heat, pour the oil and add the onions, celery, leek, carrots, and garlic. Brown the veggies up, about 10 minutes, then turn down the heat to low. Add the tomato paste, stirring so you don't burn anything. Cook 5 to 8 minutes to eliminate the paste's tin taste. Now, add your wine.

Place the brined tongues in the pot and add 4½ cups (1 L) water. Add 4 bay leaves, the remaining thyme, and the parsley. Do not season with salt—the tongues should have enough salt. We can fine-tune the seasoning later.

Bring to a boil and use a spoon to skim off any foamy scum that rises to the top. Turn down the heat to low and let the tongues bubble away in this bath for 3 hours, or until you can slide a knife easily through without any fight.

Once the tongues are ready to peel, place on a plate to cool for a few minutes so you can handle them. If you have plastic gloves, now would be a

Recipe continues

good time to use them. Using a small knife, peel the skin off the tongues. It should be very easy. We won't be using the skin for anything, so that can go straight into the garbage.

Place a large terrine mold on top of a tray so when we push down on the tongues, the liquid won't overflow onto your counters or floors. Place the tongues into the mold and shape into a "69." Ladle some of the tongue broth through a fine strainer on top.

Cut a piece of cardboard into a lid-size rectangle for the terrine mold. Wrap it in aluminum foil, then wrap in plastic wrap. Place it on top of the tongues, then place something heavy on top to weigh down the tongues; refrigerate. The tongues will join together like a soldier coming home to his family. These tongues will be forged together as the most beautiful tongue loaf!

The next day, remove the mold from the refrigerator. Drag a sharp knife along the sides of the mold. It will be filled with meat jelly. Keep all of that! We're going to warm the molds with our broiler to loosen the meat from them. Place a baking rack in a baking sheet and turn on the broiler in your oven. Place the mold upside down on the baking rack and let sit 3 to 5 minutes. It should come loose.

Pull the mold off the tongues, and you will have a beauty of a red meat loaf.

Slice thin and cold for sandwiches with lots of mustard, or slice thick and grill it or pan-fry it. It's a very versatile piece of meat. Grill over medium heat to add color and grill marks. Serve with Kozlik's if you can get it, or a nice Dijon.

Grilled Oysters

SERVES: AS MANY AS YOU
WANT; IT DEPENDS ON YOUR
HAUL FROM THE OCEAN OR
YOUR FISHMONGER. LET'S SAY
THIS IS FOR 4 FRIENDS.

PREP TIME: 30 MINUTES

24 large oysters

1 pound (4 sticks/455 g) unsalted butter, at room temperature

1 bunch tarragon, chopped

1 bunch green onions, sliced

1 head garlic, peeled and minced

1 bunch flat-leaf parsley, chopped

Kosher salt and freshly ground black pepper

1 baguette

Olive oil

2 lemons, zested and cut into wedges

1 pound (455 g) rock salt

1 bottle Tabasco sauce

I love grilled oysters. My Grampy would turn on the grill after we pulled some out of the strait. Garlic butter and crunchy bread crumbs with splashes of Tabasco are an unstoppable combination with the creamy, salty oysters. The butter will drip down your hands all the way to your elbows. As kids, my brothers and I loved seeing how much Tabasco we could splash on these bad boys. Or how many lemon wedges we could suck. Dad would always bet us to drink hot sauce, suck on a lemon, or eat wasabi for a dollar. My older brother Stephen was the king of wasabi. I just liked eating oysters.

—

Preheat the oven to 400°F (205°C). Heat a grill to medium-high. Shuck the oysters by draining off the liquid and saving the meat. Place the oysters back in the shells, on a tray; put a wet towel over them and refrigerate.

In a stand mixer or with a hand mixer, mix the butter on low so it doesn't fly everywhere. Add the tarragon, onions, garlic, and half of the parsley and mix until incorporated. Season with salt and pepper and set aside.

Cut the baguette in half crosswise, then into quarters lengthwise to make 8 strips of bread. Drizzle with oil and season with salt and pepper. Place on a roasting pan and roast in the oven until dark golden brown and nice and crunchy, about 5 minutes.

Once the bread has cooled, break it into pieces and place in a food processor; blitz on pulse. You don't want dust; you want beautiful crumbs. Place the bread crumbs in a bowl lined with paper towel and add the lemon zest.

Remove the oysters from the fridge and spoon the herb butter into the shells. Push the butter down and scrape the top flat. Once you've filled all the oysters, you're ready for the grill.

Place the oysters on the grill and close the lid. Once they start bubbling away, after 1 to 2 minutes, add a little bread crumb pile to each one. Cook for 2 more minutes.

Line a plate with rock salt (so the oysters don't spill). Place the oysters on the plate. Add the lemon wedges to the plate, get your bottle of Tabasco, and garnish with the remaining parsley.

Be careful not to burn your mouth on these puppies. They are uncompromising little heat bombs.

Mussels and Garden Vegetables with Aïoli

—

SERVES: 5
PREP TIME: 15 MINUTES

—

FOR THE MUSSELS, VEGETABLES, AND HERB SALSA:

5 pounds (2.3 kg) mussels

Sea salt and freshly ground black pepper

Olive oil

Juice of 1 lemon

White vinegar

5 baby carrots

3 to 6 heirloom tomatoes

½ head cauliflower

1 cucumber

1 zucchini

1 bulb fennel

1 bunch radishes

½ pound (225 g) green beans

1 bunch of parsley, chopped

1 bunch of tarragon, chopped

1 bunch of mint, chopped

FOR THE AÏOLI:

4 eggs

5 cloves garlic, peeled

1 tablespoon Dijon mustard

4½ cups (1 L) canola oil

Zest and juice of 1 lemon

3 tablespoons white vinegar

Sea salt and freshly ground black pepper

5 scallions, thinly sliced

1 bunch of chives

Olive oil

By the middle of August each year, Grampy's garden was at its finest: Tomatoes, runner beans, cauliflower, cucumbers, zucchini, onions, scallions, herbs, and flowers were all ready for harvesting. This dish makes for a perfect snack after a late-day swim in the ocean or after a fight with your brothers.

As a kid, you never really understand the work that goes into things like making dinner, driving your family across a province, camping, or growing a garden. This recipe takes a lot of work: getting the garden up and going, watering and taking care of it, letting your grandchildren run around, grabbing everything off the vines . . . It must have been really easy for my grandfather to let us ravage it the way we did! Ha! Grandparents are the best.

This dish might be my favorite thing to eat in late summer, when everything is just perfect. This recipe lets the vegetables shine more than the mussels. The mollusks are just little mineral jujubes to pop in your mouth after you give them a healthy dip in aïoli.

—

In a large 6-quart (5.7 L) pot, place the mussels and 1 cup (240 ml) ocean water (or water with enough salt that it tastes like the ocean) and bring to a boil. Once the mussels open, about 30 seconds, ladle them with a spider or slotted spoon into a large bowl filled with ice and salted water to chill out the plump, beautiful mussels. You always want to season your ice baths. It only makes sense, guys: Why season something, then wash away all that seasoning in an ice bath? Always season your ice baths!

Once the mussels have been chilled, place them in a bowl. Add just enough oil to coat them and add half the lemon juice and a little vinegar. Stir and season with salt and pepper; reserve.

Cutting and prepping the vegetables is all up to you. I like to keep things simple: If a carrot is long, cut it in half. If a tomato is small and round, keep it whole. Cauliflower? Just use the tip of your knife and cut into the core only; once you're close to the florets, flick the knife and break off the cauliflower florets so it still looks like a cloudy dream. Use your imagination a little with this. You want your vegetables to look natural, like they've been grown and picked the way you've cut them. Makes sense, right?

Make the aïoli: Place the eggs and garlic into a blender, add the mustard, and spin until incorporated. Add the canola oil slowly. Just let it gently stream into the blender, and soon the mixture will become rich and velvety.

Once the aïoli has turned into aïoli, add half the lemon zest and the lemon juice, the vinegar, and some sea salt. Give it another pulse or two to fully incorporate the acid and seasoning.

Scoop the aïoli into a bowl. Add the rest of the lemon zest, a pile of scallions, the chives, some pepper, and a little drizzle of good olive oil on top.

Make the herb salsa: In a bowl, place the parsley, tarragon, and mint. Add a little olive oil—just enough to coat. Don't let them drown. Add the remaining lemon juice. Stir gently and add salt and pepper. We're going to drizzle this on top of the veggies as well.

Place all the veggies on a platter, like an audience watching a Bob Dylan concert on a grassy hill. Line them up, making a rainbow of vegetables. Then bring out the bowl of aïoli and the mussels. Drizzle the fresh herb salsa over the lined-up, beautifully cut vegetables. Dip and eat away.

Grampy's greenhouse

Fried Clams

SERVES: 4
PREP TIME: 30 MINUTES

FOR THE FRIED CLAMS:

3 pounds (1.4 kg) of clam bellies or strips (fresh or from can)

1 cup (125 g) all-purpose flour

4 eggs, beaten

½ cup (45 g) ground and sifted saltine crackers

½ cup (90 g) cornmeal

2 tablespoons Old Bay Seasoning, plus more to taste

Canola oil

Freshly ground black pepper

FOR THE TARTAR SAUCE:

4 tablespoons (68 g) diced dill pickle

2 tablespoons capers, drained and finely chopped

1 cup (240 ml) mayonnaise

Zest and juice of 1 lemon

Kosher salt and freshly ground black pepper

FOR SERVING:

2 lemons, cut into wedges

Tabasco sauce

Fried clam bellies are maybe the best things ever. It's like eating delicious deep-fried morsels of briny meat. I like bellies better than strips; they are more adventurous and way tastier but might have sand, which is part of the vibe. Once a week, we'd go to Comeau's Seafood Restaurant in Pennfield, about an hour from Saint John. It's a perfect little restaurant on the side of the highway that serves breaded seafood. You can order the mixed fried seafood, but what you really want is just a pile of fried clam bellies, lots of lemon, Tabasco, and tartar sauce. The hardest part is finding cans of clam bellies. You can find them online, or hopefully you make it to a supermarket in the Maritimes or the East Coast.

Make the fried clams: Drain the clam bellies on a tray lined with paper towels and place more paper towels on top. You really want these as dry as possible.

Set up a breading station: Fill 1 bowl with ½ cup (65 g) flour, 1 bowl with the eggs, and 1 bowl with the saltine crackers, the remaining ½ cup (65 g) flour, the cornmeal, and 2 tablespoons Old Bay.

Fill a large Dutch oven with oil. Bring the oil to 300°F (150°C). Add the clam bellies to the flour. Shake off any extra flour, then add to eggs. Stir gently with a fork, then add to Old Bay–cracker mixture. Shake off any extra breading.

Fry clams in small batches so the temperature of the oil doesn't fall too much. The clams should take only 1 to 2 minutes to turn golden brown. Remove with a spider or slotted spoon onto a platter lined with a paper towel. Season with pepper and more Old Bay. Continue until all clam bellies are fried.

Make the tartar sauce: Fold the pickles and capers into the mayonnaise, then add the lemon zest and juice and season with salt and pepper.

Eat all of the fried clams with a little tartar sauce, lemon, and a few splashes of Tabasco. You could even throw these guys on a bun and make a po'boy if you wanted. The world is yours!

Lobster Roll

SERVES: 4
PREP TIME: 30 MINUTES

2 (2-pound/910 g) lobsters

1 cup (240 ml) Hellmann's mayonnaise

Zest and juice of 1 lemon

2 stalks celery, diced

2 dill pickles, diced

1 white Spanish onion, diced

½ white cabbage, shredded

Sea salt

2 cups (4 sticks/455 g) unsalted butter

4 flat-sided hot dog buns

Old Bay potato chips, for serving

Lobster rolls are sacred, and all I'll say is this: Do not toss lobster with mayonnaise, ever! A lobster roll should be a toasted, buttered, flat-sided hot dog bun overflowing with lobster. I love to add a little trail of chopped white cabbage slaw on top for crunch and maybe a little drizzle of melted butter. That's it! If you ever order a lobster roll and it comes as a lobster salad on a bun, throw that shit in the garbage and never go back to that place!

—

Cook the lobsters. See Hot Butter, Cold Lobster (page 22) for instructions.

Remove the lobster tails and claws and set aside. Take off the legs. Break the bodies in half. Take all the meat out of the lobsters. (Save the shells and make lobster bisque or broth!) Cut all the meat into bite-size pieces and place in a bowl. Refrigerate until ready to use.

Make the coleslaw: In a large bowl, combine and mix well the mayonnaise, lemon zest and juice, celery, pickles, onion, cabbage, and salt. Refrigerate until ready to use. If you want to make the coleslaw ahead of time, add the onion at the last minute—the longer it sits, the stronger the taste of the onion will get.

Prepare the lobster roll: In a small skillet set over medium heat, melt the butter until it's deep golden brown and nutty smelling, 6 to 8 minutes. Cool completely.

Set a cast-iron grill pan or skillet over medium-high heat. Brush the outsides of the buns with some of the melted butter and cook, turning once, until golden, about 5 minutes.

To serve the lobster rolls, place a spoonful of coleslaw in each bun. Top with a shitload of lobster and drizzle with the brown butter. Top with more coleslaw and serve with Old Bay potato chips.

Lobster Pie

SERVES: 6
PREP TIME: 2 HOURS

3 (2-pound/910 g) lobsters

1 pound (455 g) slab bacon

4 sprigs thyme

3 cloves garlic, peeled
(1 smashed, 2 sliced)

4 shallots, peeled and diced

1 stalk celery, diced

2 carrots, peeled and diced

2 leeks, cleaned and diced

2 tablespoons and 1 cup
(2 sticks/225 g) unsalted
butter, plus more if needed

1 cup (240 ml) white wine

2 cups (480 ml) heavy cream

¼ bunch tarragon, chopped

¼ bunch parsley, chopped

Kosher salt, enough to salt
water and potatoes

8 large Yukon gold potatoes

Leftover lobster meat is the gift that keeps on giving. Even if you don't have any leftovers from a boil, go buy more lobster and make lobster pie. This is a dish I love eating and making. It's perfect for winter nights, fall evenings, or a hot day. Fuck it: It's good anytime! Creamy leeks, shallots, carrots, celery, fresh herbs, chunks of sweet lobster, crispy salty bacon, all hidden under a bed of buttery mashed Prince Edward Island's finest Yukon golds. This is one for the books!

—

Cook the lobsters. See Hot Butter, Cold Lobster (page 22) for instructions. Clean all the meat out of the lobster claws, tails, and knuckles. This will be messy. Place the lobster meat in a bowl, cover with a wet paper towel, and refrigerate. Preheat the oven to 400°F (205°C).

Shave the skin off the bacon: Place the bacon skin side down on a cutting board and slide a knife along the very edge where fat and skin meet, like you're filleting a fish. You can keep the skin; we will use it in this recipe as a flavoring agent. Slice the bacon into lardons; transfer to a cold pan set over medium heat. Add the bacon skin. As the lardons start sweating and rendering fat, stir. Once they really start bubbling, turn down the heat to low. Throw in half the thyme and the smashed garlic. Let the bacon bubble away slowly and really render into dark little crunchy lardons. With a slotted spoon, place lardons on a paper towel–lined plate; discard the skin and reserve the bacon fat.

In a medium saucepan, combine the shallots, celery, carrots, leeks, and sliced garlic. Add 4 tablespoons (60 ml) of the bacon fat and 2 tablespoons butter and cook the veggies over medium heat till they're translucent. You don't want any color on them.

Over medium heat, add the wine and reduce by three-quarters. Then add the cream and reduce by half. Add the remaining thyme and the tarragon and parsley to the vegetables. Once the veggies are beautiful and creamy, add the bacon and remove from heat.

Boil a large pot of salted water. Peel the potatoes and leave whole; boil until fork-tender. Drain the potatoes and let steam for 3 to 5 minutes. Cube remaining butter, add to the potatoes, and whip with a hand mixer; add more butter if needed. Season with salt.

Add the lobster to the creamy bacon and vegetables. Pour the mixture into 4½-quart (4.3 L) baking dish and place the mashed potatoes on top; level flat with a spatula. You can drag a fork over the top a couple times to create some texture. Bake until golden brown, 25 to 35 minutes.

Remove from the oven and let rest for 10 to 15 minutes. Scoop onto plates and enjoy this super-rich beautiful dish!

Prince Edward Island
Seafood and Steaks

SERVES: A SQUAD OF FAMILY
AND FRIENDS

PREP TIME: ALL DAY

FOR THE COURT BOULLION:

3 heads garlic

2 bulb fennel

3 yellow onions

1 head celery

3 leeks, cleaned

2 pounds (910 g) baby red potatoes

6 ears corn, shucked

1 bouquet garni (1 bunch each thyme, flat-leaf parsley, and tarragon wrapped in twine)

5 bay leaves

Kosher salt

FOR THE SURF:

4 (2-pound/910 g) lobsters

4 (2-pound/910 g) crabs

4 pounds (1.8 kg) clams

4 pounds (1.8 kg) quahogs

2 pounds (910 g) shrimp

4 pounds (1.8 kg) mussels

Old Bay Seasoning

Ingredients continue

This is a team effort. While someone is on the seafood boil, someone will have to be cooking the big steaks. The steaks will take about 15 minutes to cook and 20 minutes to rest. So once the steaks go into the pan, drop your seafood into the boil.

When my family used to do this at my Grampy's house, we would split into teams: My brothers and I would go with Grampy and make the court bouillon, and my sister would help Dad with the steak, while Mom would be getting all the dips and breads, setting the picnic tables with newspaper and lots of paper towels. And always making sure everyone had a glass of lemonade, or some Lamb's Palm Breeze Rum (for Grampy).

These days were the best: early-morning clam digging, eating oysters out of the Northumberland Strait; picking up the lobsters and beef from local fishermen and farmers; picking the veggies from Grampy's garden; and then finally eating all this amazing food in the backyard. I highly suggest using some outdoor rocket propane burners—they are a great investment.

—

Make the court bouillon: This is the base of flavor for your seafood. Fill a 2-gallon (3.8 L) pot halfway with cold water and bring it to a boil.

Cut the vegetables into large pieces. This will allow for a long cooking time and maintain the integrity of the produce. It also makes it easy to plate when the seafood is cooked off. Cut the garlic on the bias in the middle of the head so the cloves stay together. Keep the core of the fennel intact, cut in half, then cut each half into 3 wedges. Cut the onions in half, and cut the celery in half, leaving the leaves on.

Place the garlic, fennel, onions, celery, leeks, potatoes, corn, bouquet garni, and bay leaves into the boiling water. Seasoning the court bouillon is very important. You want it to taste like a soup. Add ½ cup (120 g) kosher salt, then add more if needed. Simmer 30 minutes.

Make the surf: Add the lobsters and the crabs first; these will take about 4 minutes per pound. Add the clams and quahogs; cook 4 minutes. Then add the shrimp and mussels. After all the shellfish have opened up nice and wide and the shrimp, lobsters, and crabs have turned a beautiful red, you are good to go.

This is a dangerous part—gather the strong ones for lifting the pot off the stove or outside rocket burner and bringing it to the table. With a large spider (or slotted spoon if you're not a big-dog chef), start pulling up all the

Recipe continues

FOR THE TURF:

2 (45-ounce/1.3 kg) bone-in rib-eye steaks (côte de boeuf)

Kosher salt

Canola oil (for cast-iron pan)

3 tablespoons unsalted butter (for a cast-iron pan)

ACCOUTREMENTS FOR DIPPING AND SPREADING:

Chow-Chow (page 25)

Real mayonnaise

1 pound (455 g) unsalted butter, melted

Mustard Pickles (page 71)

Good country-style bread

Fresh vegetables

Really nice fleur de sel

bounty you've just worked so hard for. Place it on the newspaper-covered table, then once all the seafood and veggies are in a huge pile, grab your Old Bay shaker and dose everything with the best seasoning in the world. The aroma will forever be ingrained in your mind and heart.

Make the turf (on a grill; to cook in a pan, see opposite page): Let the steaks rest at room temperature for 1 hour. Heavily season the steaks with salt and get your grill as hot as you can.

Place the steaks on the grill. The second that fat starts dripping, you're going to get flames, so make sure you have a spray bottle filled with water ready to douse those flames. Also, don't be afraid to take the steaks off if the flames get a little too aggressive.

Getting a nice char is great, but don't let the steaks turn into charcoal. Moving them around is completely fine. Finding sweet spots on your grill is a natural progression of life: man versus fire.

Once you get a nice char on the outside, move all the coals to one side of the grill and place the steaks on the other side. This will be your indirect cooking debut. Now you can control how close your steaks get to the coals and therefore control the doneness of your steaks. Grill about 7 minutes per side.

Once done, tent with aluminum foil and let rest 15 to 20 minutes before slicing.

Place the sliced steak in the middle of the beautiful seafood bounty and start jamming and eating and loving. Serve with chow-chow, real mayonnaise, melted butter, mustard pickles, country-style bread, fresh vegetables, and really nice fleur de sel.

Make the turf (in a cast-iron pan): Let the steaks rest at room temperature for 1 hour. Heavily season the steaks with salt and pour ½ inch (12 mm) of canola oil in two large cast-iron pans. Set over medium-high heat.

Place the steaks in the pans. Let a nice golden brown color form. Flip the steaks and repeat on the other side.

Once you have golden brown steaks, pour off half the oil and add the butter; melt. Cook 7 to 12 minutes per side, using a spoon to baste with the butter.

Place the steaks on a rack over a baking sheet and pour the butter over the steaks. Rest for 15 to 20 minutes before slicing.

Place the sliced steak in the middle of the beautiful seafood bounty and start jamming and eating and loving. Serve with chow-chow, real mayonnaise, melted butter, mustard pickles, country-style bread, fresh vegetables, and really nice fleur de sel.

Hot Turkey Sandwich

SERVES: 4

PREP TIME: 3 HOURS AND 15
MINUTES PLUS OVERNIGHT
REFRIGERATING

2 turkey breasts

Canola oil

Kosher salt and freshly ground
black pepper

2 large turkey necks

1 onion, chopped

1 carrot, chopped

2 stalks celery, chopped

2 tablespoons tomato paste

3 quarts (2.8 L) chicken stock

2 bay leaves

1 bunch parsley (optional)

1 bunch thyme (optional)

3 tablespoons flour

2 tablespoons unsalted butter,
plus more for the peas

4 slices white bread

1 (12 ounce/340 g) bag
frozen peas

I love, love, love hot turkey sandwiches. Soft white bread, thick turkey gravy, a good mixture of dark and white meat, with frozen peas! The peas are what make the sandwich special. There's something textural about them; without peas, this sandwich would be too soft on soft. And no one wants that. With this recipe we braise the turkey necks. Adding the braised neck meat between the roasted breast is just too good not to do.

We aren't going to brine our turkey breast; we are going to cook it nicely and let it come to temperature. Resting it makes the breast juicy. This takes a day to prep, though. We have to roast the breast and braise the necks, then the following day we can make this sandwich for all the people we love.

At the Blue Goose Restaurant, Grampy always had plenty of roasted turkey breast for hot turkey sandwiches. These are best eaten in cold weather with French fries or creamy coleslaw.

—

Preheat the oven to 350°F (175°C). Coat the turkey breasts with oil and season with salt and pepper. Place the turkey breasts on a baking sheet lined with parchment paper. Roast until a thermometer inserted into the thickest part of the breasts reaches 145°F (63°C). Remove the breasts from the oven and wrap in plastic wrap. Let cool, then place in the fridge until the next day.

Meanwhile, pat the turkey necks dry and cut into 2-inch (5 cm) portions. (You can cut right through the vertebrae.) Season with salt and pepper. In a Dutch oven, heat ½ inch (12 mm) of oil over medium heat. Cook the turkey necks until they're nice and dark brown on all sides. Remove and set aside. To the same pot, add the onion, carrot, and celery until they're cooked down, then add the tomato paste; cook for 5 minutes, stirring occasionally.

Place the necks back into the pot and add the stock and bay leaves. You can add parsley and thyme as well. Bring to a boil, skim the scum that rises with a ladle, and turn the heat to low; braise for 2½ to 3 hours. Once the meat on the necks is fork-tender, remove the necks and strain the stock into a large container; refrigerate overnight.

The next day, pick the neck meat off the bones. Make the gravy: In a medium saucepot over medium heat, cook the flour and butter until golden brown, stirring constantly, 10 to 15 minutes. Add 4 cups turkey stock from the necks.

Thinly slice the turkey breasts against the grain. Place one slice of bread on a plate, then top with 3 slices of breast and 2 heaping tablespoons of the cold braised turkey-neck meat, then 3 more slices of breast. Push down on the meat to compress. Pour hot gravy over the entire sandwich. In a medium saucepan, warm the peas with just a little butter and water; season with salt. Spoon a big pile on top of your hot turkey sandwich.

Porterhouse

SERVES: 4
PREP TIME: 1 HOUR

2 (2-inch-/5 cm thick) porterhouse steaks

Kosher salt

Canola oil

3 tablespoons unsalted butter

I was eight years old the first time Grampy brought me to a cattle farm. We drove for a while down the back roads of the island. There are many backwood trails that cars and trucks still use to get from town to town. I always loved taking these back roads. I would daydream about Robin Hood when driving down them; I was Robin and would be keeping an eye out for the evil Sheriff of Nottingham, devising my attacks from behind fallen trees or swooping down from ropes tied up high in the tree branches.

But let's get back to beef. I remember seeing these long-haired Scottish cows that you see in movies like *Braveheart*. The farm was half for dairy, half for beef. I didn't even realize steak came from cows until my Grampy asked which one we wanted to eat! My brothers and I freaked out. We got to pick the cow? Grampy was just fucking with us . . . but not really. We went into the butcher shop that was attached to the farm and grabbed a couple bone-in rib-eyes.

PEI is only now getting recognized for its beef, and I think that it could be the best beef in Canada! The grass and air here make for some pretty special beef; it's very aquatic in flavor. There's only one other ranch with beef that tastes this way, and it's Bryan and Cathy Gilvesy's Y U Ranch in Norfolk County, Ontario. They raise 100-percent-grass-fed Texas Longhorns that live in pasture until slaughter.

This is how you cook a perfect porterhouse, best for eating on a picnic table in the backyard! Maybe grab a head of lettuce from Grampy's garden to wash it all down.

—

Let the steaks rest at room temperature for 1 hour. Heavily season with salt.

Heat ½ inch (12 mm) of oil in each of two pans. Place the steaks in the pans over medium-high heat. Allow a nice golden brown color to form, about 4 minutes. Flip the steaks and repeat on the other side.

Pour out half the oil and add the butter; melt. With a spoon, baste the steaks with the butter while cooking, 7 to 12 minutes per side.

Place the steaks on a rack over a baking sheet and pour the butter over the steaks. Let rest 15 to 20 minutes before slicing.

Bar Clams

SERVES: 6
PREP TIME: 4 HOURS

25 bar clams

Ice

1 loaf store-bought sourdough bread

1 cup (2 sticks/455 g) unsalted butter, at room temperature

1 jar Mustard Pickles (page 71)

Bar clams are rare, and a jar of them is one of the best things in the world. Not a lot of people really understand how good bar clams are. One of the first times I met Chef Robert Prendergast, he told me that I had to try them, so we walked around the block and he popped the trunk of his car—where he had a few coolers and boxes full of PEI seafood and shellfish. He cranked open a jar of bar clams and first he took a sip of the liquor to make sure it was up to snuff, like a fine wine. He gave me a nod and a wink and passed me the jar for a sip and to dig my fingers inside. I pinched a couple of bar clam pieces out of it. They were delicious—not too salty, not too sweet. It was a perfect jar of bar clams, at 9 A.M., out of the trunk of a car. That's a real Maritimer for you—Robert is so compelled by his seafood that the time of day doesn't even matter. It only matters that he shares something he loves so much. I'm just lucky because I love bar clams as much as he does.

Rinse the clams in a bucket or a pot in the yard with a hose. Hose water is the best kind of water to clean seafood and shellfish. In a large pot with 1 gallon (3.8 L) water, bring all the clams to a boil, until they open. Remove the clams and place in a large pot full of ice and hose water. (Shocking the clams keeps them from getting dry.)

Remove the clam meat and slice each into 5 pieces and place in a bowl. (Bar clams have bellies attached, as well—you can cut each belly into 2 or 3 pieces.) You should have about three 500 ml-size mason jars' worth of bar clam meat. Place in the fridge while you sterilize the jars.

In a clean pot, boil the jars, lids, and seals for 5 minutes, then place on a clean dry kitchen towel. Fill each jar three-quarters of the way with clams, then fill with cold water. Put on the seals and lids.

Place the jars in a pot, cover completely with cold water, and bring to a boil; turn down and simmer 1 hour. Remove the jars and place them upside down on the kitchen towel and let them cool to room temperature. Refrigerate 24 hours, and you'll have the most flavorful bar clams in the world.

To serve, slice the bread and spread with butter. Stack the drained bar clams and pickles on top. Enjoy!

Wild Blueberries and Cream

SERVES: AS MANY PEOPLE AS
YOU CAN PICK BERRIES FOR,
HOPEFULLY ENOUGH FOR 4

PREP TIME: 5 MINUTES

2 cups (200 g) wild fresh
blueberries

1½ cups (385.5 ml) good heavy
cream

Zest of 1 lemon

When my grandfather passed away, we were left with many of his belongings: his Royal Canadian Mounted Police uniform, a leather blackjack, snowshoes, animal pelts, and photos of his life. But the one thing that has always stuck out in my mind was his bucket hat. When my father came back from Prince Edward Island to Fort Erie with these heirlooms, we would sit around and tell stories about Grampy while looking at the artifacts. This dusty old bucket hat with salt stains grabbed my attention; the inside looked like it was covered in blood. This was his blueberry-picking hat, colored from years of picking wild blueberries on his walks. He would pick only a hat full, never taking more than he needed and leaving the rest for the birds he loved. That was Grampy, a true man of nature: never living in excess, never taking more than needed, always leaving some for the next person or animal to find and enjoy. On a recent trip to PEI, I filled my own hat to the brim with wild blueberries. It was a special moment for me because my hat has my son's nickname on the front. Life comes full circle.

Grampy would serve the blueberries ever so simply with just some whipped cream or maybe with some fresh vanilla ice cream or angel food cake. I loved just a bowl of blueberries and heavy cream—nothing beats that simplicity. And this recipe may be the easiest one to make in this book. All you need is time and to know where blueberries are growing wild! Good luck! May your hat always look like it's been through a bloody war and be full of blueberries.

—

Wash your blueberries in room-temperature water and let dry in a dish towel. Divide the blueberries into four bowls.

Pour the cream halfway up the blueberries and sprinkle the lemon zest on top of the berries and cream.

Savor this dish—it's one of my favorites, like, ever!

Wild blueberries forever

Molasses Bread Pudding

SERVES: 8

PREP TIME: 1½ HOURS PLUS
2 DAYS RESTING

FOR THE MOLASSES BREAD:

1 cup (240 ml) warm water

1 teaspoon granulated sugar

1 tablespoon active dry yeast

¾ cup (180 ml) molasses, such
as Crosby's Fancy, plus more
for serving

1 cup (90 g) rolled (old-
fashioned) oats

1 cup (240 ml) hot water

1 cup (240 ml) room-
temperature water

2 cups (250 ml) whole-wheat
flour (spooned in)

4½ cups (560 g) all-purpose
flour (spooned in)

2 teaspoons kosher salt

Unsalted butter

FOR THE BREAD PUDDING:

4 eggs

4½ cups (1 L) heavy cream

2 ounces (60 ml) brandy

1 teaspoon ground cinnamon

1 tablespoon grated nutmeg

2 tablespoons unsalted butter,
plus more for the loaf pans

Ingredients continue

Another Maritime institution is Crosby's molasses, made in the city of my birth, Saint John, New Brunswick. Every home has molasses on the table—it's like Maritime ketchup. On your cereal, on your toothbrush, on your spaghetti . . . Maritimers put it on everything. Growing up, we always had molasses bread for breakfast with cold butter and more molasses drizzled on top, and when we were bored with that, Mom would transform the bread into molasses bread pudding. A few loaves were made at the start of the week, and by Saturday or Sunday, Mom would be making bread pudding with that week-old dried-out homemade bread for breakfast.

Make the molasses bread: In a bowl, combine the warm water and sugar, then sprinkle the yeast on top. (The sugar helps activate the yeast.) Let sit 5 minutes.

In a medium bowl, place the molasses and oats; stir to incorporate. Using a kettle, pour the hot water into the molasses-oat mixture, then pour in the room-temperature water. Stir with a whisk, then add the yeast mixture; whisk to fully incorporate. Transfer to the bowl of a stand mixer with a bread hook. Add the whole-wheat flour slowly on a low speed (so you don't get covered in flour). Then add the all-purpose flour and salt and let it come together. Raise the speed to medium and let the dough knead 5 minutes.

Grease two 9¼ by 5¼-inch (23.5 by 13.3 cm) loaf pans with butter. Scrape the dough into the loaf pans; drape a kitchen towel over them and place in a warm area of your home for 1 hour, or until they have doubled in size.

Preheat the oven to 350°F (175°C). Place the two loaf pans on a baking sheet and bake 45 minutes, until the bread has a crispy shell and you can puncture the center with a wood skewer and it comes out clean.

Set the baking sheet on a rack and let the bread cool for 30 minutes. Remove the bread from the pans and cool even further. If you want, try a slice with some cold butter, molasses, and salt on top for a real treat. Wrap the bread in plastic wrap until you're ready to make the bread pudding.

Make the bread pudding: In a blender, mix the eggs, cream, brandy, cinnamon, and nutmeg.

Cut the molasses bread into 1-inch (2.5 cm) cubes, then fill two buttered and parchment paper–lined loaf pans with the bread and pour half the blended mixture into each pan. Refrigerate 30 minutes.

Recipe continues

1 cup (200 g) granulated sugar

½ cup (120 ml) heavy cream

2 tablespoons unsalted butter

2 tablespoons sour cream

½ teaspoon sea salt

2 cups (480 ml) heavy cream

Preheat the oven to 350°F (175°C). Bake the bread pudding for 45 minutes. Let rest for 1 hour, then wrap in plastic wrap and refrigerate 24 hours.

Make the caramel sauce: In a medium saucepan, pour the sugar and 1 cup (240 ml) water; bring to a boil, then keep boiling until it becomes golden brown bubbles. (Be careful because it's easy for the sugar to get burned.) Turn off the heat, pour in the heavy cream, and stir with a whisk. It will bubble. Add the butter and sour cream, whisking until it becomes smooth. Add the salt.

Make the whipped cream: In a stainless-steel bowl, whisk the cream until stiff peaks form, about 5 minutes. Maybe get someone with really strong shoulders or forearms, like a sister or aunt who played curling, or an uncle who was good at the classic arcade game Pac-Man.

Using a butter knife, cut around the edges of the pans and remove the bread pudding; tear away the parchment paper. Slice the bread pudding into ½-inch- (12 mm) thick slices.

In a nonstick pan over medium heat, melt the butter. Place the bread pudding slices in the pan and let them get crispy, 2 to 3 minutes per side. Serve with the sauce and whipped cream.

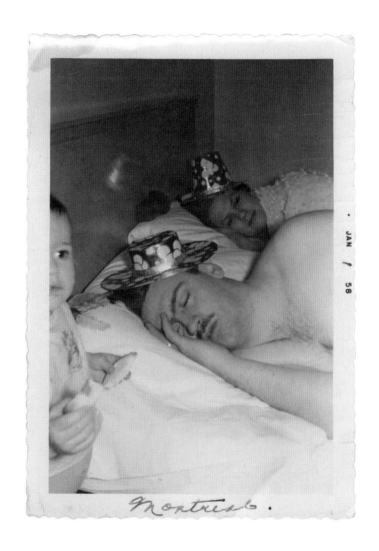

Edith and John recovering from New Year's Eve on January 1, 1958

CHAPTER 2

Lionel and Dorothea Poirier

Top: My Nanny wearing a beautiful blue dress in the kitchen of the Sea Breeze
Bottom: Grampy calling Nanny to see what's for supper

THE CHIEF DIDN'T LIKE
GETTING SOAP IN HIS EYES

Grampy Poirier was a military policeman in the Korean War. After his service, he returned to Nova Scotia to be with Nanny. It's a weird thing, some of the parallels between my mom's parents and my dad's: Nanny Poirier started a restaurant in Lockeport, Nova Scotia, called the Sea Breeze. Grampy started a taxi service and owned a theater. He eventually used his military police experience to build a long and successful career in municipal policing. Lockeport was a fish-process hub back in the day, so it was a great place to open a seafood restaurant. The people who worked in the fish plants, on the seiners and draggers, all came to the Sea Breeze for the best homestyle seafood in town. If it wasn't good and authentic, they'd let you know.

When my dad first fell for my mom, Joan, his future father-in-law was the chief of police in Woodstock, New Brunswick. My grandfather Len heard about "that Matheson boy" and didn't want his daughter hanging out with the troublemaker. Fortunately for Dad, Grampy let him after getting to know him. Despite owning a restaurant with his wife, Grampy was not a cook in any way, shape, or form. I'm not sure he ever cooked anything that did not come out of a can. He loved Nanny's cooking and ate every bit of anything she made.

Nanny Poirier is one of those wonderful, kind, and accepting people whom everyone looks up to. As a stay-at-home mom, she did all the cooking and is an amazing pickle- and preserve-maker as well. She came from humble beginnings, and her stories of hardship from her childhood are inspirational. The Chief, as tough as he was, was set in his ways: Dinner was served at 5 P.M. sharp, and Nanny had to wash his hair in the sink because he did not like to do it himself for fear of getting soap in his eyes. He, a man who survived the horrors of war and was decorated for bravery, was so afraid of getting soap in his eyes that he couldn't even wash his own hair! What the fuck, Grampy. Get it together. That didn't matter. Nanny accommodated him, lovingly washing his hair every day.

Roast Pork Loin

SERVES: 8 TO 10

PREP TIME: 1 HOUR, PLUS
OVERNIGHT RESTING

1 (12-inch-/30.5 cm long)
skin-on pork loin

4 cups (960 ml) canola oil, plus
more for rubbing

Kosher salt and freshly ground
black pepper

3 tablespoons garlic powder

Every time I smell roasting pork I think of this dish and my Nanny and Grampy Poirier. My parents never made pork, and I'm not sure why. Maybe that's why this dish is so special to me. The fattiness of the skin-on pork loin and the way the skin cracked . . . I loved it so much. Nanny always made it with gravy, roasted whole carrots, parsnips, mashed potatoes, and pickled beets. She would score the skin like I had never seen, and I never really saw again till I went to Copenhagen, where they serve the best roasted pork loins ever! Which is funny because my grandmother never went to Copenhagen. But it makes sense to slice the skin instead of scoring it in a crosshatch fashion—it's easier. This recipe is part my Nanny and part my love of one of my favorite cities in the world, Copenhagen. Serve this with your favorite vegetables, potatoes, carrots, or squash. Homemade applesauce goes well with this meal too.

—

With a box cutter, score the skin of the pork loin straight across as thinly as possible all the way down the loin, not too deep: You want to just score the skin, not the fat. Air-dry the pork overnight in your refrigerator.

The next day, preheat the oven to 450°F (230°C). Place the pork loin on a rack set on a baking sheet. Rub with oil, salt, and the garlic powder. Roast in the oven. You want it to get golden brown fast, about 15 minutes, then turn the heat down to 300°F (150°C) and cook until a thermometer inserted into the thickest part of the meat reads 135°F (57°C), about 1 hour. Remove from the oven and let rest, 25 to 30 minutes.

In a Dutch oven, heat the oil to 350°F (175°C). Place the rested pork loin (on the rack) over the Dutch oven. Now, what you're going to do is dangerous, so be very careful: Ladle the hot oil over the skin until it is fully converted into a perfect pork rind. It will crackle away and turn into the most beautiful thing you've ever seen. This is what makes this dish so perfect—the rested pork loin and the super-crunchy crispy skin. Slice into ½-inch (12 mm) pieces and season with salt and pepper.

Chicken Soup

—
SERVES: 5
PREP TIME: 3 HOURS
—

1 (3 to 4-pound/1.4 to 1.8 kg) whole chicken

Kosher salt and freshly ground black pepper

3 tablespoons canola oil

½ cup (120 ml) good olive oil, plus more for serving

2 onions, diced

2 carrots, peeled and diced

2 stalks celery, diced

2 leeks, cleaned and white parts diced

1 bunch parsley

1 bunch thyme

4 bay leaves

1 lemon

Chicken soup is something everyone should know how to make. It's one of those dishes that's healing. All you need is chicken and water. Serve it with grilled-cheese sandwiches or just by itself. It's good for breakfast, lunch, or dinner. Add noodles or rice, Parmesan cheese, or chopped kale. It's one of my favorite foods. My Nanny always made it with her leftover roast chicken dinner, a meal she cooked often. I loved knowing that after a roast chicken dinner came the chicken soup.

The real beauty of chicken soup is that it's such a blank culinary canvas. You can make Mexican pollo verde, pho ga, Italian wedding soup, broth for tortellini. It starts with roasted chicken and water and can end in any part of the world you wish. But this one is my grandmother's, and I hold it close to my heart.

—

Preheat the oven to 400°F (205°C). Pat your bird dry; season with salt and pepper and rub with the canola oil. Place on a rack set on a baking sheet and roast in the oven until the chicken is golden brown and the juices run clear when a knife is inserted between the leg and breast, 45 minutes to 1 hour.

In a Dutch oven, heat the olive oil over medium heat and add the onions, carrots, celery, and the white parts of the leeks. Cook until the veggies are tender, about 15 minutes. Stir every 3 minutes to make sure everything is cooking evenly.

Remove the chicken from the oven and drain the rendered fat into the pot with the onion mixture (also known as a mirepoix). Let the chicken rest for 15 minutes so you can handle it. Cut the chicken in half and place in the pot. Add just enough water to cover everything.

Bundle the parsley, thyme, and bay leaves and tie with twine; drop it into the pot. Bring to a boil, then turn the heat down to low and skim the scum with your ladle; simmer 1½ hours.

Remove the chicken from the stock and clean the meat and skin off the bones. Leave nothing. Chop the meat into medium dices, then return to the soup. Season with salt and pepper. You may notice you'll need a lot of salt to bring out that chicken flavor. But don't be afraid to keep adding until you reach that salty-rich broth you've been searching for your entire life.

Ladle some into a bowl and add a squeeze of fresh lemon juice or a few drops of good olive oil, and hopefully you're watching your grandfather's crow's-feet curl up as he's smiling at you.

Fish Cakes

—

MAKES: 16 FISH CAKES

PREP TIME: 3 HOURS PLUS
1 DAY SOAKING

—

1 pound (455 g) salt fish
without skin (white fish, like
cod or haddock)

1 pound (455 g) potatoes,
peeled and quartered

¼ cup (½ stick/55 g) unsalted
butter

1 egg

½ bunch green onions, chopped

Cornmeal

Canola oil

Freshly ground black pepper

Mustard Pickles (page 71),
for serving

This is another classic East Coast staple. Fish used to be the cheapest protein you could get, so it was very popular. These fish cakes are made with salted fish, which is traditional. There are many ways to preserve food, but salting is probably as old as man himself as a preservation method. The fish cakes can be frozen before you fry them, and they make a nice comfort meal you can serve quickly to brighten up a dreary, cold Sunday-morning breakfast.

—

Soak the fish in fresh water for 1 day, changing the water two or three times, to remove most of the salt.

Preheat the oven to 350°F (175°C). Drain the fish and arrange on a baking sheet. Roast for about 30 minutes; remove, drain, and let cool until you can handle it. Break the fish into small pieces by hand, discarding any bones.

While the fish is roasting, set a large pot of water to boil. Boil the potatoes 10 to 25 minutes, until tender; let cool.

With a potato masher, mash the potatoes coarsely with the butter; add the egg and combine with the fish and green onions.

Scoop a medium-size ball (about 2.5 ounces) for each fish cake, roll into a ball, and flatten into a perfect cake. Coat in cornmeal.

In a frying pan, pour about ¼ inch (6 mm) of oil and heat to 350°F (175°C). Working in batches, carefully place the fish cakes in the oil and fry until golden brown, about 4 minutes a side. Wipe the pan and replenish the oil after each batch of fried cakes. Season with pepper and serve hot alongside mustard pickles.

Mustard Pickles

MAKES: TWO 500 ML-SIZE
MASON JARS

PREP TIME: 3 HOURS

2 cups (300 g) pearl onions, sliced ¼ inch (6 mm) thick

2 cups (200 g) cauliflower, cut in ¼-inch (6 mm) pieces

2 cups (300 g) small cucumbers, seeded and sliced ¼ inch (6 mm) thick

1 cup (240 ml) white vinegar

½ cup (100 g) granulated sugar

2 tablespoons dry mustard

1 tablespoon turmeric

1 tablespoon kosher salt

½ cup (65 g) cornstarch

My mom loves to make a mustard pickle sandwich. These mustard pickles have a thick sauce and won't run out all over the place. They are excellent on hamburgers and hot dogs and make a great side with fish cakes, a boiled dinner, or a pot roast.

—

In a large pot, place the onions, cauliflower, and cucumbers. Add the vinegar, sugar, dry mustard, turmeric, and salt. Simmer gently until tender, about 15 minutes.

Turn off the heat. In a small bowl, combine the cornstarch with about 2 tablespoons water to make a slurry, then whisk the slurry into the vinegar mixture. While the mixture is hot, pour it into the Mason jars, cap them, and listen for the "doink" when the cap is pulled in by the cooling of the pickles. After about 15 minutes, test the tops with a gentle push to make sure they are sucked in. Don't worry: For any that aren't, you can refrigerate, or you can reheat and re-cap.

Store your pickles in a cool, dry, dark place; there's no need to refrigerate until opened.

Rabbit Stew

SERVES: 4
PREP TIME: 2 HOURS

2 (3 to 4-pound/1.4 to 1.8 kg) whole rabbits

Canola oil

Kosher salt and freshly ground black pepper

1 pound (455 g) slab bacon, cut into 1-inch (2.5 cm) cubes with skin removed but saved

3 cloves garlic, peeled and minced

6 shallots, peeled and diced

2 carrots, peeled and roughly chopped

2 stalks celery, roughly chopped

1 pound (455 g) cremini mushrooms, halved

1 pound (455 g) baby new potatoes

2 tablespoons Dijon mustard

2 tablespoons tomato paste

3 cups (720 ml) good dry red wine

About 4 cups (960 ml) chicken stock

1 bunch tarragon

1 bunch parsley

1 bunch thyme

1 bunch sage

Bread, for serving

Salted butter, for serving

This is one of those classic grandma dishes that everyone loves. It's usually made with chicken, but this time we'll use rabbit. Nanny always made it with rabbit. They were readily available, as everyone trapped them and used them for barter. She used to get a penny for every rabbit she skinned for Uncle Harvey.

—

Pat one rabbit dry and place on a large cutting board. Put the rabbit on its back and cut the legs off. Cut the body into three pieces, making a cut right after the ribs and then cutting the saddle (hips) into two pieces. Now do it again with the other rabbit.

In a Dutch oven over medium-high heat, pour just enough oil to cover the bottom. Season the rabbits with salt and pepper and sear them until golden brown. Remove the browned rabbit and reserve while you build the rest of the stew.

Drain the oil and add the bacon and bacon skin. Turn the heat down to low and let the bacon warm up, about 5 minutes. You don't want crispy lardons; we are looking for gently browned, tender bacon. Add the garlic and let brown just a little, then add the shallots, carrots, celery, mushrooms, and potatoes. Cook 8 minutes, stirring every 2 minutes.

Add the mustard and tomato paste and stir for another 5 minutes. Add the wine and the rabbit. Then add just enough chicken stock to cover the rabbits. Add the herbs: Tie the herbs together in a bundle and tie to the handle of the pot so you can discard with ease.

Bring to a boil, skimmng the scum that rises to the top, and then turn down the heat and simmer for 1 hour. You don't want to overcook the rabbits. They will become dry and loose. You still want a little firmness to the rabbits and vegetables. Remove from the heat, discard the bacon skin, and season with a little salt and pepper. Serve with good bread and butter.

Mussel Stew

SERVES: 5
PREP TIME: 2½ HOURS

Kosher salt

5 pounds (2.3 kg) mussels, scrubbed and debearded

Olive oil

3 cloves garlic, peeled and minced

1 onion, diced

1 stalk celery, diced

1 carrot, diced

½ bulb fennel, diced

1 (6-ounce/170 g) can tomato paste

2 tablespoons paprika

2 cups (480 ml) dry white wine

1 pound (455 g) salt pork

1 (14.5-ounce/411 g) can diced tomatoes

1 zucchini, diced

Freshly ground black pepper

1 bunch chopped flat-leaf parsley

1 bunch tarragon, chopped

Grilled bread, for serving

Nanny used to make this when times were tough and there was nothing to eat but mussels and vegetables. In her day, you didn't go hungry if you were willing to go out and harvest your food. Mussels were free on the rocks; you grew veggies in your garden. Basically: You work, you get to eat.

—

Fill a bowl three-quarters full of ice. Add water up to the top.

In a large pot set over high heat, pour 1 cup (240 ml) seawater or salted water and bring to a boil. Add the mussels to the pot and cook, until they open (should be almost instantly). Turn off the heat.

With a slotted spoon or a spider, place the mussels in the ice bath. Leave for about 10 minutes. Pick the mussels out of the shells and set aside. Reserve the mussel liquor.

In a large Dutch oven set over medium heat, pour just enough oil to cover the bottom. Add the garlic; let it become a little golden. Next, add the onion, celery, carrot, and fennel and cook until translucent.

Add the tomato paste and cook for another 5 minutes, stirring every minute or so. Add the paprika, wine, and reserved mussel liquor.

Drop the salt pork into the stew and bring to a boil, then turn down the heat; simmer 1 hour. Next, add the tomatoes and cook 1 more hour.

Add the zucchini at this point so it doesn't turn to mush. Add the mussels to the stew. Grab the braised salt pork and shred it with tongs and a fork; place the meat back in the stew.

Season the stew with salt and pepper; add the parsley and tarragon and a few drizzles of oil. Serve with grilled bread.

Pot Roast

SERVES: 6 TO 8
PREP TIME: 5 HOURS

1 (4-pound/1.8 kg) rump roast, tied with butcher twine into a uniform shape

Canola oil

Kosher salt and freshly ground black pepper

8 shallots, peeled

5 carrots, peeled

1 stalk celery, cut in half

4 leeks, cleaned and white and green parts separated, sliced

2 tablespoons Dijon mustard

2 tablespoons tomato paste

1 (750 ml) bottle good dry red wine

4 cups (960 ml) beef stock

4 sprigs thyme

½ cup (1 stick/115 g) unsalted butter

1 lemon

A good pot roast is something special. My Nanny would make this on Sundays after church. She would get the roast going in the morning, and by the time she would get home, she would just have to finish the vegetables and mashed potatoes. (We didn't have to go to church with her because we were Mormon and she and Grampy were good Catholics.)

People say that pot roast is the poor man's prime rib, and that you're either a pot roast or a prime rib family. Clash of the classes. But I feel that when done right, they are equal and both have characteristics that are strong and powerful. The pot roast is just like making a diamond: Apply a little pressure and time to that rump roast, braise it, and baste it, and you will have a beautiful broken-down piece of meat. Pot roast is also a winner because you get gravy from the braising liquid. One-pot cooking is the best: You can throw in carrots, onions, parsnips, rutabaga—all your root vegetables—and pick them out when they are cooked and then just finish the roast by reducing and basting. Nanny and Grampy Poirier were definitely pot roast people. Even though they had money and could afford prime rib, Grampy liked his pot roast on Sundays. And so did I!

—

Dry the rump roast with a paper towel; rub with oil and season with salt and pepper.

In a large Dutch oven set over medium-high heat, pour ½ inch (12 mm) of oil. Place the rump roast in the Dutch oven; rotate to make sure it becomes golden brown and glistening, not dark brown or burned. You don't want to "hard sear" the rump roast; it should be golden brown on each side and the ends. This should take 2 minutes per side. Remove the seared rump roast and set aside.

Discard most of the oil; leave just enough to sauté the vegetables. Add the whole shallots, whole carrots, celery, and the white parts of the leeks; cook gently for 5 minutes. Add the mustard and tomato paste and continue to cook for another 5 minutes.

Add the wine and stock. Return the rump roast to the pot and add the thyme. Bring to a boil and skim the scum. Turn the heat down to low and cook, covered, 2 hours. Remove the vegetables and set aside. Continue to simmer, covered, 1 hour.

Uncover, turn up the heat, bring to a boil, and cook, basting the roast frequently with a large spoon until the sauce is reduced by more than half, about 1 hour. Remove the rump roast; strain the sauce into a medium saucepan and whisk in the butter. Season with salt (if needed), a squeeze of lemon juice, and some pepper.

Place the vegetables on a platter. Cut the twine off your rump roast and slice it into 1-inch (2.5 cm) pieces; spoon the sauce over the pot roast.

Blackberry Coffee Cake

SERVES: 12
PREP TIME: 1 HOUR

1¾ cups (220 g) all-purpose flour, plus more for dusting

1 cup (200 g) granulated sugar

2 teaspoons baking powder

¼ teaspoon baking soda

¼ teaspoon salt

3 eggs

¾ cup (180 ml) sour cream

1 teaspoon vanilla extract

1 tablespoon brandy

Zest of 1 lemon

3 cups (420 g) blackberries

Unsalted butter

Vanilla ice cream, for serving (optional)

In Fredericton, where Grampy was chief of police for many, many years, my grandparents had this beautiful home at the back of a cul-de-sac. When I was a kid I thought it was a mansion. It had big white pillars, and they had blue carpets and really nice furniture, and everything was so perfect—doilies and art everywhere. Everything was always so nice and clean. I'm not saying we had a messy house or that we lived in a shack, but there were four kids in our house, always smashing things. My grandparents had a backyard that seemed to go on forever, where my brothers and I would play with our wooden toy guns. At the edge of the yard was a giant blackberry bush that was often used as a hiding spot from my two brothers rather than the culinary treasure that it was. Their house always smelled so good. I can still smell the coffee cake coming out of the oven and cooling by the back window. I can see my mother, my auntie Iris, and my sister playing some card game, my dad, Uncle Frank, and Grampy watching the Expos on TV, and my brothers and me running around everyone, trying to get their attention. I didn't include a lot of desserts in this book because I don't like to bake, but this cake is super easy and means a lot to me.

—

Preheat the oven to 350°F (175°C). Butter an 8-inch (20 cm) round cake pan and dust with flour.

In a large bowl, whisk together the flour, sugar, baking powder, baking soda, and salt.

In another large bowl, whisk together the eggs, sour cream, vanilla, brandy, and lemon zest until smooth.

Make a well in the dry ingredients and pour the wet mixture into the middle; stir until fully incorporated. Fold in 1 cup (140 g) of the blackberries with a rubber spatula.

Pour batter into the prepared pan and add the remaining blackberries. Bake about 1 hour, until golden brown and a cake tester inserted comes out clean. Let cool. Serve with good vanilla ice cream, some whipped cream, or even just a little crème fraîche. Have some tea and play cards with your grandmother.

CHAPTER 3

Mom and Dad

Left: My father as a child
Right: My mother as a child

YOU CAN'T PICK YOUR PARENTS AND
I WOULDN'T CHANGE A DAMN THING

My parents are classic high-school sweethearts. They've been together since 1973 when my mom's family moved to Woodstock, where her father was the new chief of police. Dad saw the most beautiful girl he'd ever laid eyes on and was lucky enough to make a life with her and raise four kids.

We had an active family life filled with lots of weekend camping and visits to the grandparents. We really loved getting out into the woods. One of our favorite camping spots was Cape Blomidon, Nova Scotia. It's a true wilderness experience on the Bay of Fundy, with the highest tides in the world. There's lots to do there: hiking, rock hounding, fishing, just being part of nature. And there's very little ambient light, so the stars at night are spectacular. Mom and Dad learned a lot about camp-cooking during this time and our camp meals evolved into full-on dinners with all the sides.

As us kids were growing up, Mom and Dad did a few things differently. We had no TV in the home until my youngest brother was nine. We had a stone-mill grinder. Mom ground fresh flour and baked the most amazing bread *every day*. Mom cooked turkey dinner with all the fixins almost every Sunday. Sometimes she'd make pork roast or roast beef instead. My mom's roasts were my favorite.

Her ability to turn leftovers into what we thought was a gourmet dish kept us all well fed and living within the budget of a six-member family of a risk-taking entrepreneur. This means that sometimes money was tight. Today, I'm not much of a leftovers kind of guy. I find them boring. I hate eating the same thing two days in a row. We all took turns with chores—dishes, laundry, cleaning the litter box—and we all got to work on our cooking skills. So far two of us have become good in the kitchen: my sister, Sarah, and me. The other two, Steve Jr. and Adam, not so much. I still have hope that one day their genetic code will take over and they will become decent cooks instead of living off cereal.

When I was in fourth grade, my dad started a new company, which brought our family to a new province—Ontario. We packed a moving van full of everything we owned, and the family into our Plymouth Sundance. We drove seventeen hours from Dartmouth, Nova Scotia, to Fort Erie. That drive was fucking insane. Three boys in the backseat with my sister sitting shotgun and my mom driving. My dad was in the moving van solo.

It felt like we were driving for fifty-six days straight. We cried the whole way, never to see any of our friends again. I was crushed.

We didn't even have a house when we got there. We lived in a hotel for a week until we found an amazing house to rent in Crescent Park, Fort Erie. I went to elementary school and high school in Fort Erie until I got kicked out of high school for being a mischievous idiot. That landed me at Lakeshore Catholic High School, where I met the love of my life, Trish, and some lifelong best friends.

Although at first I was crushed about moving, Fort Erie quickly became our home. We moved around a lot in the Maritimes as kids, but in Fort Erie our family was able to get grounded. We quickly became a part of the community. My brothers and I played lacrosse and baseball. In high school, our house turned into the social hub of our group. With three boys who all had lots of friends and parents with an open-door policy, at any moment there could be a large group of teenagers at our house. On the weekends, we would have parties. It was kind of like a Canadian, high school version of *Animal House*, except with the parents and their friends in attendance. The best part of that was that every Sunday during Buffalo Bills season, my dad and mom would make more food than you've ever seen in your life for the hungover psychopaths I called friends. My parents never seemed hungover and they always managed to make food for the whole fucking block.

By the end of high school, I wanted nothing more than to leave Fort Erie for the big city—Toronto. I used to hate it, especially when I would have to come back for Christmas break during cooking school. That can't be any further from how I feel now. I love it. I try to go back to Fort Erie as much as I can.

A beautiful, resilient family. Clockwise from left: "Steve Savage," "The Sister,"
"Beav," "Boney Joany," "Griz," and me, motherfucker.

Mom's Cheesy Things

SERVES: 6
PREP TIME: 2 HOURS

2 cups (480 ml) warm water

⅔ cup (135 g) granulated sugar

1¼ teaspoons active dry yeast

1¾ cups (420 ml) canola oil, plus more

1½ tablespoons salt

6 cups (750 g) all-purpose flour or whole-wheat flour

2 cups (230 g) grated Cheddar cheese

2 tablespoons Mexican chili powder

½ tablespoon cayenne pepper

1 tablespoon smoked paprika

¼ cup (60 ml) Worcestershire sauce

Freshly ground black pepper

My mom always made bread. She would even mill her own flour. Every morning, there would be a few loaves of fresh-baked white or whole-wheat bread, and most mornings we would have the bread either with strawberry freezer jam or as cheese bread with a spicy mixture on it. As kids, we loved it so much. I was, for some reason, ashamed of my big bread sandwiches at school—I always wanted Wonder Bread like all the other kids. Thinking back, I was such an idiot. I wish I had the time and patience to make fresh bread every morning for my son, let alone for four children and a husband. When I talk to Mom about her bread making now, she just laughs and says she was crazy back then. She hasn't made bread since we were in elementary school.

In a bowl, combine the warm water and sugar, then sprinkle the yeast on top. (The sugar helps activate the yeast.) Let sit 5 minutes.

Into the bowl of a stand mixer with a bread hook, pour the oil and salt; add the yeast and, slowly, the flour, 1 cup (125 g) at a time (so you don't get covered in flour), until fully incorporated. Mix 5 minutes, until the dough is fully kneaded.

Place the dough on a clean surface; cut in half and form into 2 balls. Transfer to two large bowls with some oil to make sure they don't get dry. Flip the dough to coat in the oil. Drape a warm, damp kitchen towel over the bowls and let the dough sit and rise in a warm place in your house, 1 hour. Punch the dough and let rise for another 30 minutes. Place each ball in a greased 9¼ by 5¼-inch (23.5 by 13.3 cm) loaf pan and let rise again, another 30 minutes, or until it has risen 1 inch (2.5 cm) over the rim of the loaf pan.

Preheat the oven to 375°F (190°C). Bake 45 minutes, or until golden brown with a nice crust.

Remove from the oven and let rest 20 minutes. Slice into 1-inch (2.5 cm) pieces and cover them with the cheese, chili powder, cayenne, and paprika. Place on a rack set on a baking sheet and bake until the cheese is melted. The edges should be a little burnt and the middle should be soft and chewy. Splash with the Worcestershire sauce and sprinkle with pepper.

Broccoli-Chicken Cheddar Curry Casserole

SERVES: 6 TO 8
PREP TIME: 2 HOURS

2 chicken breasts, cut into 1-inch (2.5 cm) cubes

4 boneless chicken thighs, cut into 1-inch (2.5 cm) cubes

Kosher salt and freshly ground black pepper

Canola oil

1 yellow onion, diced

1 tablespoon grated garlic

1 tablespoon grated fresh ginger

2 tablespoons unsalted butter

4 teaspoons yellow curry powder

1 cup (240 ml) heavy cream

1 cup (230 g) cream cheese

2 cups (230 g) grated orange Cheddar cheese

1 head broccoli, chopped

2 cups (630 g) frozen hash browns

1 bunch green onions, sliced

1 bunch cilantro, chopped

2 limes, quartered

There's something to be said about casserole. I'm not sure when it became popular, maybe in the 1950s, around the same time as TV dinners and the rise of Valium. Grab a bunch of meats, vegetables, and starches, and add milk, cream, cream cheese, or something else that would hold this mess together. Finally, bake it in a glass casserole dish. The sides get crispy, the cream kinda splits, and the oils run up and down the glass dish, looking like a bubbling science experiment. My mother was never an amazing cook, but she made breakfast, lunch, and dinner every day. I don't think she was a bad cook; she was more about maintaining three growing boys and a daughter on a tight schedule.

I would go to some of my Italian friends' houses and see these massive dinners with handmade pasta, seafood in tomato sauce, prosciutto-wrapped melons, veal Parmesan, tiramisu, and other foods I hadn't seen before. We were very much a meat-and-potatoes household.

This dish is one of those fail-safe meals that parents make when maybe there's a little too much going on. I grew to love this dinner. I'd never had Indian, Pakistani, or any kind of curry, but I loved this dish. I fell in love with the broccoli, chicken, Cheddar cheese, and curry cream sauce. Served with a side of minute rice, you're flying all over the world with a culinary freak flag. Every family has that one dish that your parents would make a few times a year that was misunderstood. This is that dish. It's an underdog; the original recipe was probably on the side of a can or a box, but I fell in love. It's a what's-on-the-inside kind of dish. It means well and is pure at heart.

Preheat the oven to 400°F (205°C). Season the chicken with salt and pepper. In a large cast-iron pan set over medium-high heat, pour just enough oil to cover the bottom. Sear the chicken on all sides until golden brown, 2 to 3 minutes. Remove the chicken and set aside.

Add a little more oil to the pan. Cook the onion until lightly brown. Then add the garlic, ginger, and butter. Let the butter froth and melt. Add the curry powder and stir 2 minutes. Turn down the heat to medium-low and add the cream, cream cheese, and half the Cheddar cheese; stir until fully melted. You'll see the mixture turn into a beautiful yellowy orange color.

Add the chicken, broccoli, and hash browns to the mixture; stir to combine. Pour into a glass baking dish. No need to use cooking spray—it's gonna be a mess. Sprinkle the remaining Cheddar cheese over the top of the casserole and bake until bubbling and the cheese has browned, 20 to 30 minutes.

Let the casserole rest 15 minutes—it's gonna be really hot. There's no right way to serve this. Plate, bowl, fuck—serve it out of a boot. Scoop it out, sprinkle some green onions and cilantro on top, give it a squeeze of lime, and enjoy the one dish that still boggles my mind but is so good. Trust me!

Rappie Pie: A Matheson Family Tradition

SERVES: 8 TO 10
PREP TIME: 6½ HOURS

2 (3 to 4-pound/1.4 to 1.8 kg) whole chickens, quartered

2 onions, quartered

2 carrots, peeled and roughly chopped

2 stalks celery, roughly chopped

1 bunch thyme

1 bunch parsley

Kosher salt and freshly ground black pepper

Potato base for rappie pie (page 95) or 2 frozen potato blocks

2 bunches green onions, sliced

Cooking spray

Molasses, for serving

Hot sauce, for serving

This is my family's biggest Christmas culinary tradition, and one I look forward to sharing and making with my family for years to come. We have had rappie pie every Christmas Eve. It is an Acadian dish that my Nanny Poirier learned from her grandmother. I think it should be as well known as poutine, but it has never gotten the love. I think it has to do with the fact that it's not the prettiest dish.

Everything about this dinner makes me happy: making the chicken broth, reconstituting the potato pulp that was often freezer-burnt and grayish, pouring the chicken broth, stirring the gummy potato mash back to life, and picking the meat off the braised chicken. You can buy frozen blocks of grated, drained potato from a few stores in the Maritimes, or you can make your own potato base. My Nanny would eat and make this dish a lot as a child, growing up on the shores of Nova Scotia. You could substitute mussels, rabbit, or clams for the chicken, but Nanny would never use beef. I love that this dish is served at Christmas and comes from hard times. It may seem very plain to most people, but to me, this dish is the cornerstone of my culinary makeup. This dish is family to me, it is celebration, it is tradition. And coming from a guy who has very few traditions, I hold this one close to my soul.

When we first moved to Ontario, I really missed this meal. We didn't go back to the Maritimes for almost four years when we first moved to Fort Erie. And this dish was one that always kept us connected and wouldn't let us forget our Maritime blood and history.

Please note: A rappie pie pan is a specialty item, so you will most likely have to use a deep cake pan. Do not use a glass pan; it must be a basic metal pan.

In a large pot, place the chickens, onions, carrots, and celery. Cover with cold water, bring to a boil, and skim the scum that rises to the top. Add the thyme and parsley. Turn the heat down to low and simmer 3 hours.

Preheat the oven to 350°F (175°C). Remove the chicken and let rest 15 minutes to cool so you can pick the meat off the bones. Leave the meat in large chunks—we will use all of it, light and dark. Strain all the chicken broth into another pot; season with salt until it's tasty. Set the broth to a low boil.

Now, in a very large stainless-steel bowl, place your potato base (recipe follows on page 95 if you can't find potato blocks). Add your hot chicken broth, 2 cups (480 ml) at a time, stirring it continuously with a large wooden spoon to form a dough. Keep adding chicken broth until it's smooth, like thick cake batter. If you can find the blocks, there are

Recipe continues

instructions on how much liquid to add. Basically, what liquid is taken from the potato is replaced by broth, so it's important to get that balance.

Add the green onions to the mixture. Once again, add salt until it tastes like a solidified chicken soup.

In a large well-greased (Pam works best) rappie pie pan or stainless-steel hotel baking pan, pour half the mixture. Layer the chicken on top, then layer with the remainder of the potato mixture.

Bake until you get a golden crispy top, about 3 hours. It's okay if it takes longer because you really can't overcook this dish. Remove from the oven and allow to rest 20 to 30 minutes so it's not soupy and has time to set. Cut into squares and serve with molasses, hot sauce, or plain—the way I love it. Maybe add some salt and pepper. The edges, much like a lasagna, are the most sought after. Make sure you get a corner square!

—

To make your own base for rappie pie: Peel and grate 20 pounds (9 kg) PEI potatoes very finely and then squeeze out all the liquid. What will be in that liquid? Mostly water but also a lot of starch. You must save all the liquid and starch, not to use but as a measure of what you need to put back in the remaining pulp to reconstitute it properly. It's pretty cool to see the starch settle out of the liquid. (That's what they used to use to starch shirts!)

The old-school way to do this is to peel the potatoes and put them in a bucket of water so they don't turn brown. Then finely grate a couple pounds at a time, put those gratings in cheesecloth, and wring out all the liquid you possibly can. This is very hard work.

Many devices have been made to take some of the work out of this, but today we have a machine that anyone can buy to do this: a juicer! Keep the dryish pulp for use, and keep the juice for measuring so you know how much liquid to put back. Cut your potatoes so they fit in the mouth of your juicer. Have a bowl handy to collect all the pulp and another bowl for the liquid. When all the potato is pulped, measure your liquid by volume. That is the amount of chicken broth you will add back to make the rappie pie mix.

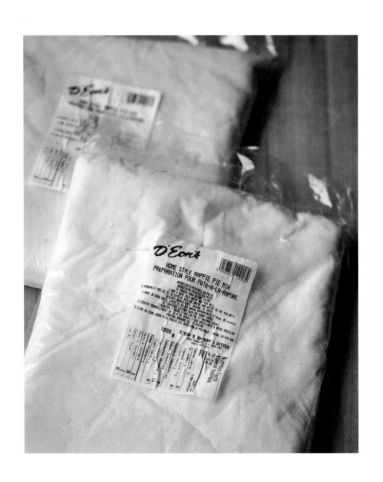

D'Eon's makes the best rappie pie blocks. It's oddly difficult to find these, even in the Maritimes.

Nanny cutting a fresh-out-of-the-oven rappie pie in the early 1990s

Roasted Goose

SERVES: 6

PREP TIME: 4 HOURS PLUS
OVERNIGHT REFRIGERATING

1 whole goose

Kosher salt and freshly ground
black pepper

10 shallots, peeled

6 cloves garlic, peeled and
halved

4 parsnips, peeled and each cut
into four spears

4 carrots, peeled and each cut
into four spears

1 rutabaga, peeled and cut
into wedges

1 turnip, peeled and cut into
wedges

15 baby new potatoes, peeled

A few sprigs thyme

3 cups (720 ml) red wine

1 cup (240 ml) chicken stock

2 tablespoons cold unsalted
butter, cubed

1 lemon

Thick berry compote, for
serving (optional)

Sherry vinegar, for serving
(optional)

I feel very lucky to have grown up eating roasted goose instead of turkey at most Christmas celebrations. There's something about that dark meat and the roasted vegetables in that golden goose fat. Goose fat is almost too good for you and definitely makes you smarter and stronger. If you had to build a house for your family during a snowstorm on the side of a mountain, this roasted goose would be the food to power you through that.

When cooking this, you might run into some small questions, like how do I not have dry breasts and undercooked legs or un-crisp skin. That's why I'm here to hold your hand and guide you through this, to make sure you finish building that house on the side of a mountain during a snowstorm with a belly full of goose. I love a roasted goose. You will love roasted goose, and you will learn how to cook this with all the love in the world. Also, save all the fat that's left over for stews, pie doughs, soups, eggs, or anything else you're going to be cooking anytime soon. It's worth more than gold! (Not really, but yeah, it is!)

—

Remove the organs, including the heart, liver, and gizzard, from the goose and refrigerate your goose, uncovered, overnight. This will allow for a very crispy skin.

Preheat the oven to 400°F (205°C) and season the goose with salt. Place the goose in a roasting pan with a rack on the bottom. Roast the goose until golden brown, 15 to 20 minutes; turn down the oven temperature to 300°F (150°C) and roast for 1 hour.

After the goose has been cooking 1 hour, you will have a lot of fat that has rendered. Drain off all the fat very carefully by taking the goose out of the oven and ladling the fat into a new baking pan. Place the shallots, garlic, parsnips, carrots, rutabaga, turnip, and potatoes in the new pan with the goose fat. Season with salt and pepper and place some of the thyme among the vegetables.

Place the goose and the vegetables back into the oven and roast another 2 hours. Cooking in that gorgeous goose fat will make the vegetables crispy and tender.

Take the goose out of the oven when a thermometer inserted into the thickest part reaches 165°F (74°C). The goose should be a dark brown with crisp skin, and the vegetables should look beautiful, all singing away in that bubbling goose fat.

Recipe continues

While you let the goose rest, you'll find some very nice juice swimming in the goose fat, and we want it for a quick pan sauce. Strain the rest of the fat into a glass container and let the fat and the goose essence separate. Skim off the fat, and you're left with just the essence.

In a medium saucepan, place the cooked shallots and a little of the goose fat and start cooking down the shallots—get them nice and caramelized, 10 minutes. Add the wine and chicken stock and reduce the liquid by half. Add the goose essence and the remaining thyme; simmer 5 minutes. Remove the pan from the heat and add the butter; stir, using a whisk, and add a squeeze of lemon juice and some salt and pepper to taste. You could serve with thick berry compote, as well as some sherry vinegar, if you're feeling like you want that fruity, tangy vibe.

Lobster Bisque

SERVES: 6
PREP TIME: 5 HOURS

FOR THE LOBSTER STOCK:

Kosher salt

6 (2-pound/910 g) lobsters, from the Maritimes or Maine

Canola oil

1 cup (240 ml) brandy

2 cups (480 ml) chicken stock

1 bunch parsley

1 bunch thyme

1 bunch tarragon

4 bay leaves

FOR THE BISQUE BASE:

1 pound (455 g) slab bacon, diced

3 Vidalia onions, peeled and diced

3 cloves garlic, peeled and diced

2 stalks celery, diced

2 carrots, peeled and diced

2 parsnips, peeled and diced

1 bulb fennel, diced

1 red bell pepper, diced

¼ cup (½ stick/55 g) unsalted butter (optional)

3 tablespoons tomato paste

4 plum tomatoes, crushed

1 cup (240 ml) Madeira wine

Ingredients continue

My dad makes the world's best lobster bisque. I still have never had a better one! He would be in the kitchen all day, just him and his bisque. My sister loved it so much that she would stand by his side and eat all the pressed mirepoix right out of the strainer, like it was the best dinner of her life. We didn't eat this all the time because buying lobsters in Ontario is like trying to buy crack from a cop . . . you get fucked! But when my dad would cook this bisque, it was his duty to make sure he got every single ounce of flavor out of those shells! This recipe is pretty much a Matheson family secret, and I didn't want to put it in the book at first, but people need this in their lives, they need it in their mouths, they need to share it with others. You need to make this bisque right now!

What is a bisque? It's a creamy seafood soup that's made with only crustaceans. Anyone who calls any creamy soup "bisque" is ridiculous and annoying. You can't make cauliflower bisque or red pepper bisque or cod bisque—you can only make bisque with shelled seafood. So, get the fuck over it with all that bisque nonsense. This is the bisque to end all bisques. Please take your time and please take this seriously. This is a Matheson treasure.

—

Make the lobster stock: Bring a large pot of water to a boil for blanching the lobsters. Add enough salt so the water tastes like the ocean. Once the water is boiling, add 2 lobsters at a time and cook for 4 minutes. Place cooked lobsters in a salted ice bath until fully chilled. Cooking the lobsters for 4 minutes will only par cook them and will make sure your lobster meat is perfect when you add it to the bisque.

Twist and pull the tails off the bodies. To catch all the juices and essence, pull off the claws over a bowl. Cut the tails into halves lengthwise and crack the claws open using the heel of your chef's knife, cracking down on the claw just enough and making sure not to cut all the way through. The goal is to keep the claws whole and cube the tail and knuckle meat. A good pair of kitchen shears is very useful for removing the tails and knuckle meat. Put the meat into the bowl and place your perfect claws on top; cover with a wet paper towel and refrigerate.

Place another large pot over medium-high heat; add just enough oil to cover the bottom of the pot. With the shears, cut all the shells into 1-inch (2.5 cm) pieces; add to the pot and cook 5 minutes, stirring every minute or so. Now you're going to deglaze with the brandy. It should flame, so be careful. If it doesn't, use a long kitchen match and ignite the brandy. Reduce the liquid by half, then add the chicken stock and 3 cups (720 ml) water and bring to a boil; skim the scum. Add the parsley, thyme, tarragon, and bay leaves. Turn the heat down to low and simmer for 1½ hours. Set the lobster stock aside.

Recipe continues

101

4 cups (960 ml) heavy cream

2 tablespoons cayenne pepper

1 cup (240 ml) brandy

1 cup (2 sticks/225 grams)
unsalted butter

Kosher salt and freshly ground
black pepper

Make the bisque base: Place the bacon in a Dutch oven set over low heat. Let the bacon start rendering fat, until almost crisp, then add the onions and garlic. Cook 5 minutes in the fat, then add the celery, carrots, parsnips, fennel, and red bell pepper. If you need to add butter you can as well. I always do. Cook 1 hour on low, until all the veggies are cooked down and caramelized.

Add the tomato paste and tomatoes and cook 5 minutes. Now, add the wine and reduce by half. Pass all the juices from the bowl with the lobster meat through a sieve to make sure there are no shells or dirty guts. Add to the pot and cook 30 minutes to let this base really come into itself.

Now strain your lobster stock into another container. You have to really smash the shells through a sieve with a ladle to get all the good stuff. Discard the shells and herbs. Return the stock to the pot and reduce by half, then add to your lobster bisque base. Bring to a boil, skim, and turn down to a simmer; cook 1 hour. Then strain this, and once again, really work all the vegetables and bacon for all you're worth. And what you're left with is the real beginnings to the best lobster bisque.

Finish the lobster bisque: Reduce your bisque one more time by half, about 20 minutes, then add the cream, cayenne, and remaining brandy; simmer 15 minutes. Stir in the butter till the bisque is silky smooth.

Add the lobster meat to the bisque and cook 5 minutes. Season with salt and pepper. Ladle into bowls and let your mind be blown.

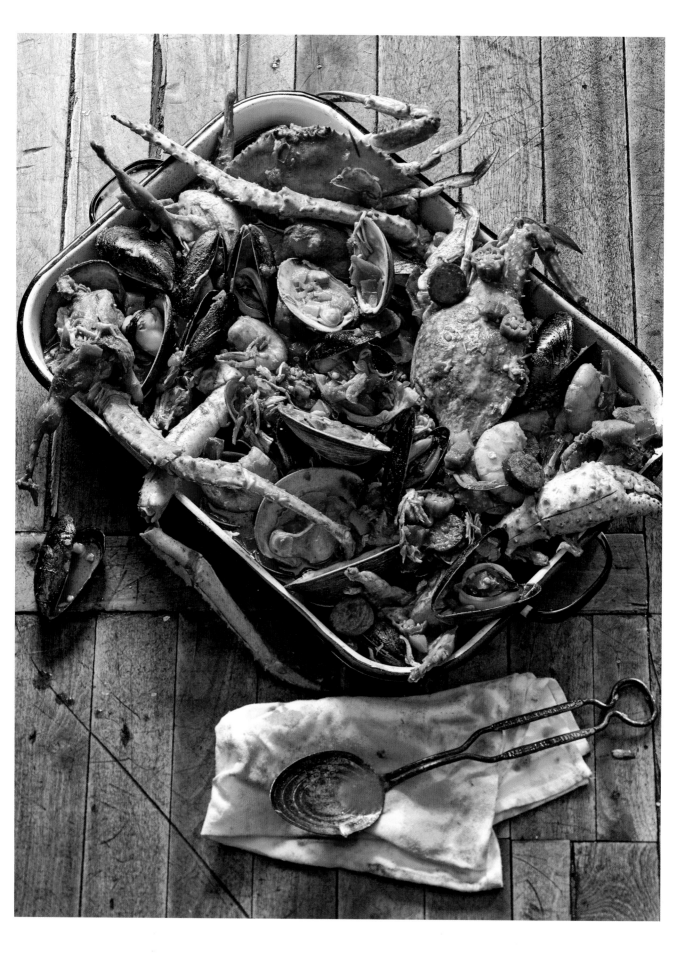

Scumbo: Dad's Gumbo

SERVES: 6
PREP TIME: 3 HOURS

2 cups (4 sticks/455 g) unsalted butter

1 cup (125 g) all-purpose flour

½ cup (120 ml) duck fat

2 pounds (910 g) andouille sausage, cut into ½-inch (12 mm) slices

1 pound (455 g) slab bacon, cut into 1-inch (2.5 cm) chunks

3 yellow onions, finely chopped

1 green bell pepper, chopped

1 red bell pepper, chopped

1 jalapeño, chopped

2 stalks celery, chopped

4 cloves garlic, peeled and sliced

3 tablespoons tomato paste

2 tablespoons cayenne pepper

4 tablespoons filé powder

2 tablespoons Cajun seasoning

2 cups (480 ml) white wine

1 gallon (3.8 L) chicken stock, plus more if needed

2 large turkey necks, cut into 2-inch (5 cm) pieces

6 quails

½ cup (120 ml) Tabasco sauce

½ cup (120 ml) white vinegar

2 whole crabs

4 king crab legs

1 cod fillet, cut into 3-inch (7.5 cm) pieces

2 pounds (910 g) shrimp

3 cups (465 g) okra, trimmed and sliced

2 pounds (910 g) clams

2 pounds (910 g) mussels

Sea salt and freshly ground black pepper

This gumbo is another one of my dad's favorite things to make. It's one of those dishes that really speaks to me. We would always have it in the summer. There's something addictive about eating a hearty soup like this when it's hot out. Seafood, sausages, poultry, and a spicy broth made with lots of love makes for layers of flavor. I add lots of extras to it, like crab, turkey necks, quails, and large chunks of andouille sausage.

You are only as good as your roux. Take your time to cook your flour and fat. It takes time and maintenance—you need to really pay attention and cook that roux until it's dark and beautiful.

A few years ago, I went down to the Tabasco factory on Avery Island in Louisiana and it blew my mind. I made a version of this recipe for the higher-ups there, and they said it was one of the best they had ever had. Either they were being nice, or it was perfect, like I thought it was. Be warned: The spice levels can lead to an out-of-body sweating experience.

—

In a large Dutch oven over medium heat, melt the butter until bubbling and frothy, then add the flour. Cook this roux with a watchful eye and whisk constantly to make sure the flour doesn't stick to the bottom of the pot, 15 to 20 minutes. Making a good dark chocolate–colored roux is very important to this dish.

In a second large pot, place the duck fat, sausage, and bacon. Cook over medium heat to render all the fat, 5 to 10 minutes. Add the onions, bell peppers, jalapeño, celery, and garlic; cook until tender and caramelized, about 10 minutes. Add the tomato paste; cook 5 minutes, stirring constantly. Next, add your spices (cayenne, filé, Cajun), then deglaze with the wine.

Slowly add 4 cups (960 ml) of the chicken stock to your roux. Use a whisk to stir, making sure there aren't any clumps of flour. After well combined, add your vegetable-and-sausage mixture. Next, add the remaining chicken stock, and you'll be left with a very nice red fatty soup. It shouldn't be thick, so add more chicken stock, if needed.

Drop the turkey necks into the gumbo and cook 1 hour over medium-high heat, then add the quails whole and cook another 45 minutes. Add the Tabasco and vinegar and cook 10 minutes.

Each type of seafood cooks for a different amount of time: First, add the crabs and crab legs and cook 5 minutes, then add the cod and cook 5 minutes. Add the shrimp and okra and cook another 5 minutes, then add the clams and cook another 3 to 6 minutes or until they open. Finally, add the mussels and cook another 1 minute or until they open. Discard any shellfish that doesn't open, and season with salt and pepper. Serve.

Ronco Rotisserie Prime Rib

SERVES: 8 TO 10
PREP TIME: 2 HOURS

1 (7-bone) prime rib

1 cup (240 ml) canola oil

Kosher salt and freshly ground black pepper

Prime rib is the best meal ever! Cooked right, it has so many amazing layers: the salty crust; the tender and broken-down outer deckle, much like pot roast; the fat that almost turns to bone marrow after being properly rested, and the eye! You get four different textures and tastes with prime rib, and I think that's why I love it so much. You never get bored with it. It keeps you coming back for more. Just when you think you can't eat more, it sucks you back to wipe up that last bit of gravy, mashed potato, or maybe even that little au jus–soaked Yorkshire pudding.

My father loved prime rib as well, and we were lucky enough to have a Ronco rotisserie oven. It was magical. I used to watch the turning piece of beef more than I'd like to admit. There's something about the rendering fats coating the salty meat mass and just turning and turning and turning. It really mesmerized me—like I was a young Mowgli looking into Kaa's eyes, being lured into the snake nest! I can smell the roasting meat as I'm writing this. It's just one of those things that fills the house and demands respect. I love prime rib. Don't be like my dad: Do not over-cook this beautiful piece of meat, and be sure to let it rest before slicing and serving.

Prime rib is easy to make, even without a Ronco rotisserie oven, and you shouldn't be scared to take on this massive, intimidating piece of meat. This may be one of the easiest recipes in this book: You salt it, roast it, and then rest it!

—

Preheat the oven to 500°F (260°C) or set on the prongs of your Ronco. Rub the entire prime rib with the oil. Season heavily with salt—be very liberal here. If you feel it's a lot of salt, add a little more. Then season with a smaller but still healthy amount of pepper.

If you are using your Ronco, just set it and forget it. We want to roast this bad boy until it hits 120°F (49°C) for medium rare (about 15 minutes per pound).

If you are using your oven, place the prime rib on a rack on a baking sheet and roast till dark golden brown, about 10 minutes. Turn down the heat to 300°F (150°C) and cook 1 hour, or until a thermometer inserted into the thickest part of the meat reads our desired 120°F (49°C).

Remove from the Ronco or oven and wrap the prime rib with plastic wrap like it's a newborn baby. Keep wrapping till it's airtight. Let rest 45 minutes. Cut off the plastic wrap and slice. You're welcome.

Caution: The top, back, sides and glass become hot
Precaucion: Las partes superior y trasera, los lados y el vidrio se calientan
Caution: Hot Surface
Precaucion: Superficie Caliente

The Spencer Family

Top left: Bill and Carol on their honeymoon
Top right: Grandpa Delduca curing soppressata at home
Bottom left: Carol making pizzas for Tricia's birthday
Bottom right: Sunday Gravy with (from left) Judy Spencer, Sarah Leary, Skye Leary, Deanna Spencer, Shannon Leary,
and my Tricia (in glasses). The Leary girls are Tricia's lifelong friends and neighbors in Fort Erie.

THE SECOND FAMILY I NEVER THOUGHT I'D HAVE

The first time I met my father-in-law, Bill, he was cleaning his eaves troughs. Trish yelled, "Hey, Dad! This is Matty, the guy I'm going to prom with." Right away I sensed he was eccentric from the way he went *mmhmmm* and briefly looked down at me over his glasses while throwing muck on the ground. He quickly turned away and continued to clean. And then Trish and I walked into the house, where Carol, Trish's mom, was making her Sunday gravy. Carol greeted me with a hug and welcomed me into their home. Right away I started hanging out there a lot. The house on Bertie Bay was filled with delicious and then-unknown food. I found out later it was Italian. Carol taught me a lot about Italian Canadian food, about which I knew nothing. Her style of cooking came from her parents, who came from Italy—Mario (who changed his name to Meyer when he came to Canada) and Louise Delduca.

My favorite thing ever during high school was waking up at the Spencer house, hungover after parties at my house. They would always have all the windows open and the sound of the great Lake Erie was amazing. Trish and I would eat cold Italian leftovers in the dining room. In the next room, after doing his chores, Bill would put on his favorite: *007* movies. None of that Pierce Brosnan shit; Bill was a Sean Connery man.

Trish was the youngest of four sisters—Rebecca, Judy, and Deanna—and a brother, Mark. All of them (except Mark, LOL) were moved out by that point, but every Sunday the entire family would be at the house to eat. We would always have a salad to start, with Italian bread. In the winter, we would have soup—Italian wedding soup if we were lucky. Most of the time it would be roasted prime rib with potatoes or Sunday gravy with spaghetti. If it was your birthday you got to pick what Carol would make. Now I get to ask, but back then I didn't, so I would convince Trish to request chicken cacciatore. I love that fucking thing. We always finished with dessert, coffee, and tea. Right away they made me feel like part of the family.

To this day, Carol orchestrates elaborate afternoon pizza parties for her grandchildren, and sometimes even for the adults. During Easter, the younger kids hunt for hundreds of plastic eggs filled with candy throughout their property. Boxing Day brunch is an epic event with more than forty family members in attendance every year. Carol is a beast in the kitchen. Trish and I still go whenever we can. There isn't a greater place to bring up a kid. Mac gets to run around on sandy beaches and in the woods like I did. I feel blessed. It's amazing—for eighteen years I've had two families that I truly love and respect.

Chicken Cacciatore

—
SERVES: 6
PREP TIME: 1½ HOURS
—

Olive oil

8 chicken legs

Kosher salt and freshly ground black pepper

1 cup (155 g) Cerignola olives, pitted

1 Vidalia onion, diced

1 red bell pepper, diced

8 cremini mushrooms, sliced

3 cloves garlic, peeled and sliced

1 cup (240 ml) chicken stock

4 cups (960 ml) Sunday Gravy (page 119) without the meat

1 tablespoon dried oregano

1 tablespoon dried red chile flakes

1 pound (455 g) linguini pasta

This is one of Trish's favorite dishes from when she was a little girl, and it became one of my all-time favorites the second I tasted it. Carol makes this dish about twice a year and uses canned mushrooms. Although I love her version, I feel using fresh mushrooms is better. Trish and her siblings disagree, but I'm gonna stand my ground on this one. It's another dish for which we can use our homemade red sauce as the base—but the sauce is a little looser than regular red sauce. We braise the chicken legs in the red sauce and chicken stock to make for a beautiful hearty meal.

—

In a Dutch oven, pour ½ inch (12 mm) of oil and set over medium-high heat. Season the chicken with salt and pepper and place in the pot. You should fit three to four legs; don't overcrowd the pot. Sear until the chicken is golden brown; remove, set aside on a plate, and repeat with the remaining chicken.

Place the olives, onion, bell pepper, mushrooms, and garlic in the pot; cook until caramelized, about 10 minutes. Add the stock and reduce the liquid by half, about 15 minutes. Add the chicken back to the pot and cover with the gravy. Add the oregano and chile flakes. Bring to a slow boil, then turn down the heat to low; simmer 30 minutes.

Bring a large pot of salted water to a boil. Cook the pasta as the label directs. This pasta cooks very quickly—to ensure you get al dente noodles, do not walk away once you drop your noodles. Drain the water. Place some noodles on a plate. Remove two chicken legs from the pot. Shred the meat and toss into the noodles. Divide the noodles onto 6 plates and top each plate with one chicken leg. Ladle sauce on top. Boom—you've got a beautiful chicken cacciatore.

Sunday Gravy

SERVES: A LARGE ITALIAN-
IRISH FAMILY AND ONE WHITE
KID FROM THE MARITIMES

PREP TIME: 5½ HOURS

1 loaf day-old bread, torn into small pieces

1 cup (240 ml) milk

1 pound (455 g) ground beef

1 pound (455 g) ground veal

1 pound (455 g) ground pork

2 cups (200 g) freshly grated Parmesan cheese

1 cup (100 g) freshly grated Pecorino-Romano cheese

½ cup (70 g) peeled and minced garlic, plus 1 cup (145 g) whole garlic cloves, peeled and sliced thin

1 handful chopped flat-leaf parsley

1 cup (100 g) dry bread crumbs

4 eggs

2 tablespoons dried red chile flakes

Kosher salt and freshly ground black pepper

Olive oil

2 pounds (910 g) Italian sausage

2 racks (2 pounds/910 g) pork ribs

½ cup (15 g) tomato paste

6 (28-ounce/794 g) cans tomato puree

1 pound (455 g) any shape pasta

Grated Parmesan cheese, for serving

This is something I loved eating when I first started dating Trish. Her mother is Italian Canadian and comes from a long line of amazing cooks from Calabria. I never had real Italian food until I met Trish. Maybe that's why I was so in love with her initially. It was her mother's cooking! I remember the first time I was allowed to help make this meal. Her mother watched me like a hawk soaring in the bright blue sky, searching for trout. If I did something wrong, she let me know right away with a slap on the hand. If I overworked the meatballs, she would make a comment that cut deep. This was before I went to cooking school—I was just an eager kid looking for the secrets to this dish. A red sauce is the foundation of every Italian family, and it was a privilege to help. I had a duty to make the best meatballs I could so I didn't let down Carol and Bill and the Spencer family. Making this sauce is like painting: You need to know when to stop. It's a powerful sauce that still needs restraint.

I used to think that spaghetti sauce had green peppers and mushrooms in it. It took me a long time to understand the power in simplicity. This sauce is the cornerstone to most of the dishes in this section; once you've made this sauce, you can add it to so many dishes. When I make it, I like to take out all the meat and divide the balls, ribs, and sausage in containers and cover with just enough sauce. Then you can take as many of these little gems as you want and reheat for days to come, or you can make little bundles of meat and sauce and freeze for a special day. Serving the meat on a massive platter and then tossing fresh spaghetti in the sauce and topping with fresh grated Parmesan is the way to go!

—

Line a baking sheet with lightly oiled parchment paper.

Soak the day-old bread with just enough milk. You don't want soupy bread; you want milky bread.

In a large bowl, place all the ground meat and mix with your hands so it's incorporated. Next, add the cheeses, minced garlic, parsley, bread crumbs, eggs, chile flakes, milk-soaked bread, salt, and pepper. This is the fun part: Deep-dive your hands into the meatball mixture, and with your fingertips, disperse all the ingredients evenly, using your full arm to reach down to the middle and flip the mixture. Imagine you are a human bread mixer. Keep pushing down and knead it almost like a dough. Once it is truly mixed, you'll know—it will look like a piece of beautiful meat marble, with the cheese, parsley, and garlic all glistening through like rock layers.

With lightly oiled hands, roll the meat mixture into perfect 2-inch (5 cm) balls, making sure they are worked just enough. Do not squish the balls— just keep rolling so they stick together. Place on the prepared baking sheet. Drape a kitchen towel over the balls as you roll so they don't air-dry at all.

Recipe continues

In a large heavy pot, pour ½ inch (12 mm) of oil and set over medium heat. Sear the meatballs on all sides. As each ball is fully browned, remove and place on another baking sheet until needed. In the same pot, sear the sausages, about 8 minutes. Set aside.

Cut the ribs into 2-bone pieces and season with salt and pepper; sear them, about 5 minutes per side. You will find that there is a lot of crisp golden meat on the bottom of the pot. This is called fond. This is the gold.

Turn down the heat to low—there is enough residual heat to get the garlic cooking. Add the sliced garlic to the pot and cook until golden brown. Then add the tomato paste; cook 5 minutes to cook out the tin flavor and develop the rich, deep flavor tomato paste is made for.

Add all the meat and the tomato puree. If it's a little thick you can add just enough water to make it easier for you to stir the meat. You don't want it too thick right now, as it's going to cook at least 3 hours, and as it cooks, it will concentrate. We will cook it to the consistency we desire.

Don't turn the heat to high to bring it to a boil. We have to bring it up slowly to make sure nothing burns. It may take almost an hour to start bubbling and simmering the way we want it to. Once it starts simmering, turn down the heat even lower. Stir the pot gently, making sure not to break up the meatballs. Cook 3 hours.

Bring a large pot of salted water to a boil. Cook the pasta as the label directs; drain and return to the pot. Ladle in enough sauce to coat the noodles—you don't want this to be saucy. Place the pasta on a platter, then ladle extra sauce into another bowl for those who want more sauce. Remove the meat and place on top of the pasta; add more sauce. Top with cheese.

Baked Rigatoni

SERVES: 4
PREP TIME: 1½ HOURS

½ pound (225 g) ground pork

½ pound (225 g) ground veal

½ pound (225 g) ground beef

1 egg

1 cup (100 g) freshly grated Parmesan cheese

½ cup (50 g) dry bread crumbs

1 handful chopped flat-leaf parsley

Kosher salt

10 turns freshly cracked black pepper

1 tablespoon dried red chile flakes

2 tablespoons peeled and minced garlic

Olive oil

8 cups (2 L) Sunday Gravy (page 119) without the meat

2 (16-ounce/455 g) boxes dried large rigatoni

2 balls mozzarella cheese, one cubed and one shredded

This is an incredible dish made straight from the heart. Crisp, burnt rigatoni edges; melted mozzarella cheese; rich, sweet tomato sauce; and little meatballs all nestled inside this beautiful mess. Dishes like this are low risk and high reward. Carol and Trish make different versions of this, and now I make my own too. How many renditions of this dish are out there, I have no idea: Every nonna or nonno or Italian American or Italian Canadian parent has his or her own version. Some may add basil leaves, dried oregano, more Parmesan, maybe even some Asiago, or all-pork balls, all-beef, or a combination or the holy trinity: veal, pork, and beef. I want to make you my version, which is inspired by my mother-in-law and my lovely wife.

I had another mind-blowing experience the first time Carol made this for me. I thought pasta was powdered cheese and overcooked little noodles that were mixed with water instead of milk or cream, and not even a nice little knob of heavenly butter. But then I saw this bubbling, glowing, cheesy casserole coming out of the oven like a newborn rigatoni baby, and it was instant love. I knew I would fight for this dish if anyone ever disrespected it—I would stand behind it like an overprotective uncle who's had one too many brown pops at a little league baseball game. I hope that when you pull this casserole out of the oven, it's one of those moments like seeing the Sistine Chapel or the ocean for the first time.

—

Place all the ground meat in a large bowl. Crack the egg on top and add the Parmesan, bread crumbs, parsley, 2 teaspoons salt, the pepper, chile flakes, garlic, 4 tablespoons (60 ml) oil, and 2 tablespoons water. Mix with your hands—make sure to dig deep with your fingers and use your shoulders to really work the mixture.

Line a baking sheet with parchment paper. Place two spoons in a cup of water; use one spoon for scooping and the other for scraping off. Make sure to dip your spoons into the water every other scoop. Scoop 1 tablespoon meat and scrape it onto the baking sheet; make little rows until done. Lightly coat your hands with oil and form the meat piles into perfect little balls.

Preheat the oven to 400°F (205°C). In a Dutch oven, pour ½ inch (12 mm) of oil and set over medium-high heat. Place the balls in the pot, but don't overcrowd the pot. Brown the meatballs in batches and place on a rack while you build your casserole.

We are going to build the casserole hot so it just has to brown in the oven. In a small pot, heat the gravy. Meanwhile, bring a large pot of salted water to a boil; cook the pasta until al dente. Check the pasta every few minutes

Recipe continues

to make sure you're not overcooking. Because we are baking in the oven, we don't want mushy noodles! We want perfect rigatoni.

Drain the pasta and pour most of it into a 9 by 13-inch (23 by 33 cm) baking dish, then add enough sauce to cover the noodles and stir. You don't want the casserole soupy and you don't want it dry; you can always add, but you can never take away. That's why I like building this by eye once all the ingredients are ready: You can add more sauce, meatballs, and rigatoni depending on your tastes. Stir the cubed mozzarella into the casserole, then add as many meatballs as you want. Stir to evenly disperse everything, then cover with a few ladles of sauce and the shredded mozzarella. Bake 20 minutes, or until the edges are almost burnt, the cheese is golden brown, and the sauce is bubbling. Remove from the oven and let rest 10 minutes.

Baked Shells

SERVES: 4
PREP TIME: 1 HOUR

Kosher salt and freshly ground black pepper

About 27 large dried pasta shells (about 14 ounces/400 g)

Extra-virgin olive oil

4 cups (980 g) ricotta cheese

½ cup (50 g) freshly grated Parmesan cheese

½ cup (50 g) freshly grated Pecorino-Romano cheese

1 handful chopped flat-leaf parsley

Zest of 1 lemon

3 eggs

4 cups (960 ml) Sunday Gravy (page 119) without the meat

Salad and Green Olive Dressing (page 126)

Making red meat sauce and baking beautiful ricotta-filled pasta shells is literally one of the best things in the entire world. The simplicity of this dish is unparalleled . . . well, maybe aside from a *cacio e pepe* or *aglio e vongole*, but those are traditional dishes, and this is just another North American Italian staple that stands the test of time. The first time I ever ate this, it was cold. Trish and I came home to Fort Erie late one night and Carol said there were some shells in the fridge. I was like, WTF are shells? Seashells? I had no idea what power was hiding in the fridge that night. Eating red sauce and baked cheese-filled pasta cold is perfectly normal. I love eating cold pastas. I'm not a huge fan of leftovers. This dish is best hot and crispy out of the oven, obviously, but what I'm saying is you can eat it the next day cold, and it's like another dish altogether. You are getting two treats with this one.

I love the way Carol cooks: She takes her time, she tastes for seasoning often, she cuts green onions with scissors, and she always makes enough red sauce for many, many meals. What I really learned from her is restraint in cooking—it's what you leave out of the recipes. These baked shells are so easy to make. I hope you eat them for breakfast, lunch, and dinner for the next two days.

—

Preheat the oven to 400°F (205°C). Bring a large pot of salted water to a boil. Cook the shells until just shy of al dente, about 10 minutes, and place on a baking sheet lined with parchment. Using your fingers, rub them with a little oil so they don't dry out. Set aside.

Place the ricotta in a large mixing bowl. Add the Parmesan and Romano, the parsley, lemon zest, salt to taste, and lots of pepper. In a small bowl, beat the eggs, then pour over the cheese mixture and mix until the zest and parsley and pepper are all living in harmony.

Stuff the shells with the ricotta mixture using a spoon. Make sure to really pack it in. You want full, fluffy baked shells.

In a 9 by 13-inch (23 by 33 cm) baking dish, pour 1 inch (2.5 cm) red sauce (Sunday Gravy), then place the stuffed shells all lined up, like kids waiting for ice cream. Make three rows, side by side. Then add a nice ladle of sauce over each one, then drizzle some oil over them as well, and maybe a little more pepper.

Bake until bubbling and golden brown, about 30 minutes. Hopefully there are some burnt edges on the shells; that's where the gold lies. You can also turn on the broiler for a few minutes to get the shells extra crunchy, but make sure to stay close because they will burn quickly. And you don't want to ruin something so beautiful!

You can serve this dish right away: Just spoon a few shells onto a plate and serve with a nice light salad tossed in green olive dressing.

Green Olive Dressing

SERVES: 4
PREP TIME: 10 MINUTES

1 cup (155 g) pitted Cerignola olives

1 clove garlic, peeled

1 green onion, chopped

Zest and juice of 1 lemon

½ cup (120 ml) extra-virgin olive oil

1 shallot, diced

1 bunch parsley, leaves chopped

3 tablespoons white vinegar

½ cup (120 ml) canola oil

Kosher salt and freshly ground black pepper

Green-leaf lettuce

This is my favorite salad dressing of all time, and it's made by my mother-in-law, Carol. I love the simplicity of it: this olive dressing on green-leaf lettuce. That's it! The very first time I went to my future wife's house for dinner, her mom served this salad. It was perfect. And I'm a guy who hates salads (not because of the vegetables, but because no one knows how to make a proper salad). Salads should be good lettuce with good light dressing, not every vegetable in the world shredded and covered in poppy-seed–honey dressing with a cup of granola or something.

—

In a blender, pulse the olives, garlic, green onion, lemon zest and juice, and the olive oil multiple times, until it becomes frothy and lumpy, like a tapenade. Keep pulsing—don't just leave it on blend. You don't want it to emulsify. Pour into a bowl.

Add the shallot and parsley to your dressing, then add the vinegar and the canola oil. Add salt and pepper to taste.

Serve the dressing atop crunchy, well-washed green-leaf lettuce (Little Gem works well too).

Left: Bill's blender, the sketchiest fucking piece of kitchen equipment I've ever seen in my life
Right: Dr. William Spencer's very organized workshop

Dr. William Spencer's Dried Pepper Flakes

MAKES: ONE 500 ML-SIZE
MASON JAR

PREP TIME: 1½ MONTHS

1 pound (455 g) jalapeño chiles

1 pound (455 g) Scotch bonnet chiles

1 pound (455 g) green serrano chiles

1 pound (455 g) red serrano chiles

1 pound (455 g) bird's eye chile pepper

Dr. William Spencer is my father-in-law and a dentist. I've had the pleasure of him fixing my broken teeth on more than one occasion. He has a wealth of knowledge in topics that range from World War I to the making of the movie *The Birdcage,* starring Robin Williams and the other guy. The thing I love about him the most is his love for spice! He has a raw jalapeño by his side at every meal and takes bites throughout. I thought that was so sick. Bill and Carol always had amazing home-made dried pepper flakes. Bill would say, "Just a pinch! Just a fingertip's worth!" He didn't want anyone overusing it or being careless with it. It is very spicy and very special. It tastes fruity and spicy, and it's my all-time favorite dried chile. I use it for so many recipes—I add it to a tomato sauce, sprinkle a little on some nice burrata over a citrus salad . . . This stuff can go on anything.

I've had the privilege of making this atomic powder only once. When Bill asked me to come downstairs one hot summer afternoon, I was like, okay, what's happening now? Do I have to help fix the sump pump or was he going to show me his *007* LaserDisc collection again . . . but no! It was to help pulverize all the dried peppers he keeps in wicker baskets down there. He handed me a bandana and goggles and said I would be needing them. He had set up some thirty-year-old blenders on top of a chest freezer. He began to explain how dangerous this was and that I needed to be very careful. He's a pretty serious guy, so I was oddly nervous in this situation, staring at my future father-in-law wearing goggles and an old bandana around his face. He looked like an insane doctor who was cooking meth in his basement. I strapped on the goggles and wrapped my face with the bandana and was like, okay, how bad could it be?

We began to blend these peppers and everything was fine until we opened them up at the same time and it was like a fucking mustard bomb went off. I mean, I was fucked! A huge reddish cloud puffed up into my face. I instantly started coughing, and within two minutes, everyone in the house was crying and coughing. Bill didn't warn anyone, so Carol and the kids started yelling, "Dad! What are you doing?" Everyone acted like a storm was coming off the lake, batten-down-the-hatches-type shit because opening the door and the windows and using towels and fans to move all the air around only made it worse. It was insanity! And I felt so bad because I was Bill's right-hand man on this pepper-gas bomb!

What I'm trying to say is to make sure you have all the windows open, or even better, grab a long extension cord and do this outside. There's nothing better than peppers that have dried naturally over a few months and all that fruity heat that concentrates into something that will last quite some time. But I get into trouble every time I make it at home, when I forget to tell Trish I'm about to drop the gas bomb!

—

Place the chile peppers in a wicker basket in a dry place, preferably by a sunny window, and allow to dry for at least 1½ months. Every week, give the basket a shake; discard any chiles that are getting moldy.

Once they are completely dried, all shrunken and hard like a maraca, they're ready. Be very careful: Wear goggles and something over your mouth. You do not want to get this in your eyes. Rip the stems off and blend in a blender until dust. It's very easy—just dangerous and time-consuming!

Italian Wedding Soup

SERVES: 6
PREP TIME: 2½ HOURS

1 pound (455 g) ground beef

½ pound (225 g) ground veal

½ pound (225 g) ground pork

5 eggs

1 cup (100 g) freshly grated Parmesan cheese

1 cup (100 g) dry bread crumbs

3 cloves garlic, peeled and minced

½ bunch parsley, chopped

Kosher salt and freshly ground black pepper

Canola oil

4 quarts (3.8 L) chicken broth

2 onions, diced

1 stalk celery, diced

1 carrot, peeled and diced

1 bay leaf

1 cup (100 g) freshly grated Pecorino-Romano cheese, plus more for topping

1 cup (45 g) fresh bread crumbs

Olive oil, for topping

Nothing beats chicken soup (except maybe an Italian sub). Learning how to make this soup isn't difficult—I want you to know how easy it is. I want everyone in the world to taste this Italian wedding soup. My wife likes to make it a few times a year, and when she does, the house fills with the amazing smells of chicken soup, browned meatballs . . . and love.

—

Place all the ground meat in a large bowl with 2 eggs, the Parmesan, the dry bread crumbs, garlic, some of the chopped parsley, ½ teaspoon salt, and lots of pepper. Mix with your hands until fully incorporated.

Line a baking sheet with parchment paper. Put a little canola oil on your hands and tightly roll as many 1½-ounce (40 g) meatballs as you can. (You should get about 20 balls.) Place on the baking sheet, then refrigerate.

In a large pot, pour in the broth and bring to a boil. Add the onions, celery, carrot, bay leaf, and a few sprigs of parsley; simmer 1½ hours. Strain and discard the vegetables.

In a large sauté pan over medium-high heat, heat enough canola oil to cover the bottom. Working in batches, add the meatballs and cook, turning, until lightly browned on all sides, about 5 minutes total per batch. Bring the broth back to boil and place the browned meatballs in the stock; simmer 15 minutes. You can also drop the meatballs directly into the broth instead of browning them first; simmer 30 minutes to cook through.

In a bowl, beat the remaining 3 eggs and add 10 turns of the peppermill, the Romano cheese, and the fresh bread crumbs; mix with a fork until it looks like cold, lumpy porridge, then add to the soup and stir. Cover for 5 minutes and the lace will be cooked.

Spoon the soup into bowls and add some chopped parsley and Romano cheese, and a little drizzle of good olive oil.

Sausage and Potatoes

SERVES: 6
PREP TIME: 2 HOURS

6 large Yukon gold potatoes

3 pounds (1.4 kg) ground pork shoulder

1 pound (455 g) ground pork back fat

½ cup (70 g) peeled and minced garlic

4 tablespoons cayenne pepper, plus more to taste

4 tablespoons paprika

3 tablespoons toasted fennel seed

4 tablespoons dried red chile flakes, plus more to taste

4 tablespoons kosher salt

25 turns freshly cracked black pepper

1 handful chopped flat-leaf parsley, plus more for serving

Hog casings packed in salt, soaked in cold water for 1 hour and rinsed well

Canola oil

2 large Vidalia onions, peeled and cut into wedges

1 lemon

Making sausages is tough, but with a helper it can become a few hours of absolute bliss. This is the dish that Trish makes the most, and it's the one that I love the most. I love everything in this book so much it makes me sound disingenuous, but let me tell you, I love all these dishes.

If you don't want to make sausage you don't have to. Just buy good Italian sausage from a butcher like a normal human being. No one has time to do something like this, or who even has a sausage stuffer or meat grinder. Why is this even in this book? Do people even cook from cookbooks?

—

Bring a large pot of salted water to boil; add the potatoes whole and cook 15 minutes. Remove from the water and place in a bowl; cover with plastic wrap. Allow the potatoes to fully cool—you can even do this the night before or, if you plan to make this at night, cook the potatoes in the morning. Once they are cool, peel them using a butter knife and a kitchen towel; cut into nice wedges. We precook the potatoes so they get super crispy when we roast them with the sausages. If you were to cook the potatoes fully and peel them hot and add them to the roasting pan, they would get stuck and fall apart.

To make the sausages, place the ground pork and fat in a large bowl; add the garlic, cayenne, paprika, fennel seed, chile flakes, salt, and pepper and mix with your hands to get it incorporated the best you can. The more you mix, the better—get your hands nice and dirty, squeeze the pork sausage through your fingers, making a fist. Add the parsley and give it one more squeeze and mix. Now, heat a small pan over medium heat and add a little sausage ball; press it flat like a mini burger and cook to taste for seasoning. These are spicy, so you can add more or less spice by adding more or less cayenne and dried chile flakes. If you enjoy the sausage and you find it doesn't need any more seasoning, it's ready to stuff into casings.

Place the mixture covered with plastic wrap in the refrigerator until you are ready to stuff. It's easier to stuff when your meat is cold.

Soak the casings in warm water until soft and pliable, at least 1 hour. Run lukewarm water through the casings to remove any salt. Tie a double knot in one end of the casing, then cut off a length of casing. Gather all but a couple of inches of the casing over the nozzle of the sausage stuffer or funnel. Start pressing the sausage mixture through, supporting the casing with your other hand. Pack the sausage as tight as you can but not to the point of bursting. When you have filled almost all the casing (or used up all the stuffing), slip the casing off the nozzle. For a coil, tie the sausage where

Recipe continues

the stuffing ends. To make links, pinch the rope and twist in alternating directions at the indentations. Randomly prick the casings with a thin toothpick or the tines of a fork to release any air that's trapped. Sausage making is a fine art and will take some time to master. We could have just bought some hot Italian sausages from the market, but that's not us anymore—we're cooks!

Preheat the oven to 375°F (190°C). In a large baking dish, generously coat the potatoes in oil and roast in the oven 30 minutes. Add a bunch of sausages and the onions and cook until everything is nice and golden brown—the potatoes are perfectly crisp and the sausages are dripping beautiful red oily juices, about 15 minutes.

Remove from the oven and place a few sausages, potatoes, and onions on each plate; squeeze some lemon juice and add a little more parsley, salt, and pepper.

Bologna Bowl

SERVES: 1
PREP TIME: 2 MINUTES

4 slices bologna

1 slice American cheese

1 egg

1 tablespoon margarine

2 slices white bread, toasted

Maldon salt and freshly ground black pepper

What the fuck is a bologna bowl, you ask? Well, it's a perfect breakfast that may or may not be good for you! You can make it as fast as you can peel back that American cheese slice and crack an egg. I had this at Trish's house back in high school, and it's been made a few times a year ever since. I think Carol started making these because raising five kids is pretty time-consuming and this breakfast yields zero pots to wash and is a complete hit with any kid. I've publicly posted about the bologna bowl only once on Instagram, and it was a fifty-fifty split of joy and complete disgust. I feel this is a dish from the times of TV dinners and microwaves, before açai bowls and kale smoothies with chia seeds or shops where you can hook an apparatus up to your nose to smell grass and bananas . . . I love this dish, and I'll defend it forever. I want to share this with you and everyone in the world, and I urge you to make this. It may not be too healthy, but let me tell you—my wife was raised on this, and she is one of the most powerful, smart, caring, driven, successful people I know. So there!

In the bottom of a microwave-safe bowl, place the bologna, then lay the cheese slice right in the middle, then crack an egg into the bologna-and-cheese cradle.

Place the bowl in the microwave and zap 45 seconds. Microwave another 30 seconds if the egg isn't cooked.

Spread the margarine over the toast evenly and cut each into 3 long slices for dipping into the yolk. Sprinkle with salt and pepper. Enjoy this for the rest of your life, ya freaks!

PART II

Cooking School and Restaurants

CHAPTER 5

Humber College

Nineteen years old, just back from Hellfest, lots of merch. In my natural habitat: dorm room, beer in hand, Piebald hoodie, listening to Jane Doe

Top left: My dorm at Humber on the fourth floor, third window on the left
Top right: The ol' murky Humber River
Bottom left: The student kitchen at Humber College
Bottom right: My literal nightmare: being trapped in a glass cage surrounded by sugar sculptures

DROP ACID, NOT SCHOOL

I moved to Toronto in the summer of 2000 for culinary school at Humber College in North Etobicoke. I got accepted into culinary school only because anyone can who has the money. My parents were on vacation the day I moved into my dorm so my dad's best friend had to move me. His name is Johnny CC—"CC" not for a motorcycle, but for his love of Canadian Club. He's a mechanic in Fort Erie and loves the song "Black Betty" by Ram Jam. He's what you'd call a "beauty"—total Canadian good guy. Beauty can be derogatory or positive, depending on how you use it. For Johnny, it was the latter. I love Johnny like an uncle.

We filled up his Chevy 454 SS with all my belongings, which were pretty much hardcore records, band shirts, and a few pairs of cargo shorts. We were off on our 170-kilometer drive to Toronto from Fort Erie. I was so stoked to be moving away from our small town. Halfway into the drive we stopped for lunch at a highway stop in Stoney Creek. When we went back to the truck it wouldn't start. We had to wait to get towed back to Fort Erie, where we unpacked and repacked into another vehicle and started the whole thing over again. At that point I didn't even care; I was so over the whole fucking day.

We got to the dorm, checked in, got my meal plan card and my residential ID card, and loaded all my shit into a very small room with a single bed, a bar fridge, a window, and a small desk. The room had painted white brick walls, and it was just a few feet bigger than a jail cell, from what I remember. I instantly plastered the walls with hardcore music posters, like of the bands Every Time I Die, Poison the Well, All Out War, and Earth Crisis. I set up my record shelf and record player.

I didn't know a soul. Once I had my shit all set up, I hugged Johnny good-bye and he left. I sat in my room listening to Converge very loudly, and within minutes a residence hall person came to my room to tell me to turn my music down. I was the crushed—I thought this was my room, and I could blast my music all day. I was like, Fuck this place, so I went for a walk and met some dudes in the cafeteria who asked if I wanted to smoke some weed. That was biggest mistake ever! Smoking weed with random people who are connected only by the fact that they are lonely and want to escape is something I should have never been a part of. We got so high I felt like I was gonna die. We walked down to this ravine behind the dorm, and I felt like I was on the set of *Jumanji*. I became very self-conscious and pretty much just ran back to my dorm room and watched *Twin Peaks* until I could breathe again. I hate weed—it's my least favorite drug!

Cooking school was intimidating to me at first. Class was supposed to start at 8 A.M., five days a week, but our chef would lock the door at 7:45. If you were locked out, that meant you wouldn't be allowed in the classroom. If you missed three classes in a semester, you would be kicked out of the program. Coming from high school, where I would skip almost every other class, this was a huge hurdle for me to overcome. But I had to—I wanted to make my parents proud and to focus on school. I wanted to be better.

I had this amazing chef-instructor named Anthony Bevan, who was this giant Irishman and who was very intimidating at first. I won him over quickly because I was an amazing chef from day one—which meant I was good enough with a knife, and I wasn't a complete dummy. Culinary school was filled with people of all ages, ethnicities, and skill levels. I loved that you were rated purely on the end result. If I made a clear, uncloudy stock I got good marks; if I made hollandaise that didn't split I got good marks; if I could butcher a rabbit I got good marks. For the first time in my life I was getting good grades. I was building self-esteem by being on time and showing up ready with clean whites, sharp knives, and the willingness to learn.

In my second year, I had a German chef-instructor named Juergen Lindner, who was missing a thumb. He told me at first that he lost it when he escaped from Nazis during World War II. Later he said he jumped ship and swam to Ireland, and a shark bit it off. I think he liked freaking out the younger chefs. He did, actually, save the tip of my pinky. I was cutting chives; my pinky got in the way, and I cut the tip off. He knew how to quickly calm a naïve, young chef. He grabbed my wrist tight and walked me to a spice blender; he poured some black peppercorns into it and then ground them. Next, Juergen poured the ground peppercorns into a bowl and told me to shove my bleeding pinky into them. It hurt like a motherfucker, but I trusted Chef. I asked why, and he told me because he didn't have any gunpowder. WTF, this chef was the real deal. I learned a lot from that day—his calmness during my duress still stays with me. Whenever a chef I'm working with is cut, burned, or injured, I am always there to hold a bleeding finger, add egg whites to a burn, or quickly drive to the ER. The minerals in the peppercorns stopped the bleeding. I wrapped my pinky with a few bandages, and I went back to cutting my chives.

In my final few months of culinary training I had this hard-ass pastry chef-instructor, McFadden. Pastry was so difficult for me. I hated it. I had to learn so many techniques that I just didn't understand. I think that's why there are so few pastry chefs, because it's actual science. It's not as simple as roasting bones, adding water to them, and having stock. This was the toughest course in the program. I was drowning in a frothy sea of buttercream, marzipan, and pâté à choux. It was the first time that cooking didn't click for me, and it made it that much easier to leave school. When my best friend's band—At the Mercy of Inspiration—asked if I wanted to tour Canada for a few weeks, I jumped at the opportunity. If you've ever read *Get in the Van* by Henry Rollins, you know what I'm talking about. Traveling with your best friends in a van can be the best thing in the world. So I left culinary school to drink beer and drive across Canada with my best friends in a stinky, shitty van.

I couldn't let my parents know I dropped out of school. There were only three weeks left in my program. So punk, right? I still have no regrets for never finishing, and I'm laughing to myself because I'm writing a fucking cookbook! I don't think everyone should drop out of school; it was just my path. It took a lot of failure to get to where I am now. My mom found out not long after and didn't tell my dad. Years later in 2009, in the first profile of me in the *Toronto Star*, written by Ivy Knight, I mentioned that I dropped out of college to tour with a metal band. My dad was like, Wait . . . so, you don't have a diploma? You may wonder how I got away with never having a conversation about graduation—my parents happened to be on a trip to Mexico so they would have missed it anyway. I always told my dad it was a great day and was sad he missed it, LOL.

CHAPTER 6

Le Sélect Bistro

Me at twenty-two with Rang. Also, the top of Allison's head. I love you, Allison.

Left: Vicky is the angel who gave me my first shot in the restaurant industry.
Right: The outside of Le Sélect

MY FUNDAMENTALLY FRENCH
FOUNDATION

When I got back from tour, I created a resume with my fake-ass college degree as the only thing on it and printed about twenty-five copies. Who wouldn't want to hire me. Then, I started walking around downtown Toronto, literally entering restaurants and handing my resume to the hosts without asking to talk with the chefs. Also, I was walking in during mid-lunch rush, which is the worst rookie move. I waited a few days for some chef to call me up and say, You got the job! When can you start? But no one called.

I'd already hit a bunch of restaurants on King Street, so I went to Queen Street. This was in 2003, so Queen Street and Spadina Avenue were still cool, and there was this bar I used to drink at all the time called the 360. Right next door was this bistro called Le Sélect. It seemed too fancy for me to work at, and I didn't want to get caught by my punk friends going into this fancy French restaurant. I had to really pump myself up to walk into this place. I saw only rich-looking people going in there. I would be drunk next door and it would be just mad adults with dresses and camel-hair coats hanging over their shoulders, ya know. I went early in the morning right before the lunch rush and knocked on the door. I was greeted by an angel named Vicky. She had this amazing smile and was so sweet to me right off the bat. She told me that she would be sure to give the chef my resume. I didn't know it at that time, but Vicky was the wife of Jean-Jacques Quinsac, who was one of the owners of Le Sélect and a master sommelier. I got a call the next day from Brad Clarke, the chef of Le Sélect. He asked if I could come down for a "stage"—a trial run in the restaurant world—at 9 A.M. the next day.

I showed up at 8:30 with my full chef uniform: checks, chef jacket, neckerchief, and tall hat. I walked inside and I was met by a Vietnamese man named Rang, who looked me up and down and asked if it was Halloween. I was like, What the fuck are you talking about, I'm here to cook. I followed him into the kitchen, my nose quickly filling up with the amazing smells of veal stock simmering and chicken bones roasting, and where a man was butchering a whole lamb. I felt a rush like from no drug I've ever done before, along with complete fear. Rang told Brad to "get this fat boy to chop parsley." Brad told me to take off my neckerchief because I'd get made fun of.

I worked my ass off to become a sous chef within two years at Le Sélect. We would do more than two hundred covers a night with only four cooks on the line. It taught me how to be a good line cook, which meant being organized and efficient, and how to "get it on"—Rang's way of urging us to keep cooking. Cooking the restaurant food became second nature. Le Sélect moved because our twenty-five-year lease on Queen Street was up and they hiked up the rent. We reopened with a new, fancy French chef. After nine months of working seventy-two hours a week for a chef who was exploiting the restaurant, I had to move on. Thankfully, after I left, Albert Ponzo became the chef, got it on track, and made it the restaurant it was meant to be in its new space. It's a truly timeless and iconic bistro. It's perfect.

Top left: Ratnam has been at Le Sélect for more than thirty-five years. One time the chefs told me to call him
a Sri Lankan word I didn't understand, and he gave me a flying knee to the chest.
Top right: One of the greatest kitchens I ever worked in. I loved cooking on this Molteni.
Bottom left: The café at Le Sélect
Bottom right: Ana has been the pastry chef at Le Sélect since day one, thirty-seven years and counting. I miss her lemon tarts every single day of my life.

French Onion Soup

SERVES: 4
PREP TIME: 4 HOURS

1 cup (2 sticks/255 g) plus 2 tablespoons unsalted butter

½ cup (120 ml) canola oil

5 red onions, sliced ¼ inch (6 mm) thick

5 Vidalia onions, sliced ¼ inch (6 mm) thick

5 yellow onions, sliced ¼ inch (6 mm) thick

Kosher salt and freshly ground black pepper

15 shallots, peeled

2 cups (480 ml) Madeira wine

1 cup (240 ml) port wine

1 cup (240 ml) sherry wine

10 cipollini onions, peeled and sliced

20 red pearl onions, peeled and sliced

4 quarts (3.8 L) beef stock

1 bunch thyme

2 bay leaves

1 loaf good sourdough bread

2 pounds (910 g) good Emmental cheese

French onion soup is onions, beef stock, crostini, Emmental cheese, and Madeira wine. This version takes more time than you'd think. But what you can do with these ingredients is so powerful and explosive. A proper French onion soup should make every bad thing in your life disappear instantly. It's a dish that will hold you tight and tell you everything will be okay when the world is burning itself to death.

When we used to make French onion soup at Le Sélect, it was all about cooking the onions for as long as we could. We used red onions, yellow onions, Vidalia onions, and shallots. Cooking these onions really low and slow makes the best soup. You want all those natural flavors in the onions to develop and caramelize over four hours. That sounds like an insane amount of time, but if you cook them for this long, you'll reap the benefits.

One time, another cook and I had an onion-cutting race. We divided a fifty-pound bag of peeled onions in front of us, set the clock, and boom—we were off, slicing like madmen! Back then, I could cut a full bag of onions in less than ten minutes. I was almost halfway done when I cut the front of my left index finger right to the bone! The blood started pouring all over the onions. I knew I'd get in trouble for doing something stupid because now I'd have to leave the kitchen and not work that night, and all the crew would hate me because they'd have to cover my dumb ass. So off I went to the hospital to get this pale snail-like piece of finger stitched back, if that was even an option. (For a few seconds, I thought I could just super-glue my finger back on and continue to work.) Anyway, nine stitches later, I went back to work the next day to make sure that onion soup was perfect!

This soup transforms from caramelized onions to one of my all-time favorite soups instantly. The cheese is just as important: Don't buy the cheap cheese; buy the best Emmental you can find, and make sure to buy great bread to make your crostini so it stands up to the rich broth and melting cheese. The crunchy bread must stand the true test—it pulls the whole dish together.

—

In a large Dutch oven over medium-high heat, heat 1 cup (2 sticks/ 225 g) butter and ½ cup (120 ml) canola oil. Add the red, Vidalia, and yellow onions; season heavily with salt. It will take some time to cook down—you need to leave the onions alone a few minutes so they start steaming and cooking. Then stir and let steam. You'll see it takes about 15 minutes for these raw sliced onions to cook down. Be sure to stir them every few minutes.

Once the onions are translucent, turn down the heat to low; this is where the patience comes into play. Stir every few minutes until the onions start to caramelize. Add the shallots. Cook on the lowest heat possible for as long as you can without burning the onions. You'll find that a lot of sugar comes out of them and they may stick. You can add a little bit of water if necessary.

Recipe continues

Once the onions are dark brown (almost like an old mop) and caramelized, after almost 2 hours, they're ready for the wine. Add the Madeira, port, and sherry, then stand back because the mixture may ignite. If it doesn't, use one of those long matches and flambé the wine.

Add the cipollini and red pearl onions. Reduce the wine by half, then add the stock, thyme, and bay leaves. Cook 1 hour and check for seasoning. Add salt and pepper to taste.

Now for the crostini: Preheat the broiler. Take that bread and, using a ring mold, cut out four circles that are the same size as the bowls you're going to serve the soup in. In a medium pan set over medium heat, melt 2 table-spoons butter; fry the bread circles like a grilled cheese but take it a little further—make sure the bread is super golden brown. Season with some salt and pepper and place on a paper towel–lined plate.

Remove the bay leaves from the soup. Ladle into oven-safe bowls, place the crostini on top, and add a big pile of cheese. Place the soup on a baking sheet and broil on the middle rack so the cheese melts and turns golden brown and bubbly but doesn't burn. Remove the soup and have at it!

Roasted Chicken with Whelk and Mushroom Beurre Blanc

SERVES: 4
PREP TIME: 2 HOURS

1 heritage chicken

Kosher salt and freshly ground black pepper

3 pounds (1.4 kg) whelks in the shell

1 tablespoon plus 1 cup (2 sticks/225 g) unsalted butter

Olive oil

1 shallot, peeled and diced

1 pound (455 g) mushrooms, cleaned with a toothbrush and quartered, with stems

½ cup (120 ml) white wine vinegar

3 sprigs thyme

1 bay leaf

1 bunch parsley, chopped

1 bunch tarragon, chopped

1 bunch chervil, chopped

Juice of ½ lemon

Zest of 1 lemon

This is the chicken to end all chickens. The best French-farmed chickens are typically a little tough, which I love. They have strong, lean leg meat from living a wonderful life of running around the French countryside feeding on grains and breathing fresh mountain air. I could be completely wrong as well—I've only been to France once.

Cooking a proper roasted chicken is easy, and you need to account for the carryover cooking from the point you take it out of the oven. I like cooking my chicken until a thermometer inserted into the chicken reads 135°F (57°C), then letting it rest: You'll always be left with a nice juicy chicken. When we roasted chickens at Le Sélect, we would season only with salt and never add any fat to the birds so that the skin would be as crisp as possible.

The sauce that we will make here is super easy and goes so beautifully with the bird. The mineral taste of the whelks, the earthiness of the mushrooms, the richness of the butter sauce, and the brightness of the tarragon, parsley, chervil, and lemon add up to a beautiful dish.

You have to make sure that the mushrooms are in season and the whelks are fresh in the shell. Only buy the best for this dish. Nothing beats fresh, powerful wild mushrooms—I love them so much. And you should be able to find whelks in Chinatown or at a really good fish shop. I get mine from Newfoundland, and they are probably the best I've ever had.

Preheat the oven to 350°F (175°C). Pat the bird completely dry and season with salt. Place the chicken on a wire rack over a baking sheet. Roast the chicken 40 minutes, or until a thermometer inserted into the middle of the breast reads 135°F (57°C).

Bring a large pot of salted water to a boil. Make sure to add enough salt to make it taste like the ocean. Prepare an ice bath. Place the whelks in the boiling water; cook 3 to 5 minutes, then place them in the ice bath to stop the cooking. Once they are cold, using a small seafood fork, carefully pull out each whelk from its shell. Some have a small shell attached to the face, as well as intestines and waste product; cut off with a knife, then rinse the meat under cold running water. Slice each whelk into 4 or 5 pieces; place in a bowl, cover with a wet paper towel, and refrigerate.

Set a medium saucepan over medium heat; melt 1 tablespoon butter and 1 tablespoon oil. Cook the shallot until translucent. Add the whelks, chanterelles, vinegar, thyme, and bay leaf. Reduce by half. Turn the heat down to low.

Recipe continues

Cube the remaining butter and whisk into the wine-mushroom-whelk mixture using a spoon and swirling the pan to emulsify the sauce into a beurre blanc. As the sauce comes together, add the parsley, tarragon, and chervil to the sauce; the whelks and chanterelles should be beautifully covered with the beurre blanc. Add the lemon juice, sprinkle in the lemon zest, and season with pepper and salt. Remove the bay leaf.

Let the roast chicken rest at least 20 minutes. Remove the two breasts and the legs and wings. Slice the breasts into 3 pieces each. Cut into where the thigh bone and leg connect. You should have 6 pieces of breast, 2 thighs, 2 wings, and 2 legs. Divide into equal portions on 4 plates and pour sauce.

Cassoulet

SERVES: 6

PREP TIME: 4 HOURS PLUS
24 HOURS REFRIGERATING

FOR THE DUCK CONFIT:

Zest of 1 orange

10 cloves garlic, peeled

1 small bunch parsley

5 bay leaves

8 sprigs thyme, roughly
chopped

½ cup (120 g) kosher salt

¼ cup (50 g) granulated sugar

6 duck legs

4 cups (960 ml) duck fat

**FOR THE BRAISED LAMB
SHANKS:**

2 lamb shanks

1 onion, halved

1 leek, cleaned and dark green
part removed, roughly chopped

1 carrot, peeled and roughly
chopped

1 stalk celery, roughly chopped

1 tablespoon kosher salt

FOR THE CASSOULET:

½ cup (120 ml) duck fat

1 pound (455 g) pork belly,
cut into 2-inch (5 cm) chunks

2 stalks celery, finely diced

1 onion, finely diced

1 carrot, peeled and finely diced

1 leek, cleaned and finely sliced

Ingredients continue

I'm writing this recipe on the coldest day of the year in Toronto. It's 9°F (-23°C) with windchill. I wish I had a cassoulet right now—it's the perfect dish for cold weather. I like making food to warm you physically and spiritually. This cassoulet will allow your body temperature to rise and your mind to open to the beautiful world that is beans and a variety of delicious meats. Cassoulet is something I feel every cook should know how to make—you have to know how to cure, to make sausage, to braise, to soak your beans (never use canned beans for a cassoulet), and to build a dish from the ground up. There's a lot of talk about whether to put tomato in a cassoulet. I think there are a few things that you absolutely need: duck confit, lamb shank, pork belly, Toulouse sausage, and large white navy beans. Other than that, you can use tomato paste, rosemary, thyme, chicken stock, or whatever you want. Cassoulet is like Bolognese in Italy; it changes from house to house, block to block, and town to village to city. But get one thing straight: You'd better put bread crumbs on top and bake that bean-and-meat mixture in that delicious duck fat until golden fucking brown.

—

Make the duck confit: In the bowl of a food processor, place the orange zest, garlic, parsley, bay leaves, thyme, salt, and sugar. Pulse until the mixture (the cure) is finely chopped and evenly combined.

Place the duck legs flesh side up in a large dish. Pat the cure onto the duck. Cover with plastic wrap and place in the refrigerator 24 hours.

Rinse off the duck with cold water, then pat dry with paper towels. Preheat the oven to 325°F (165°C).

In a Dutch oven set over medium-low heat, heat the duck fat until liquified. Carefully immerse the duck in the fat. Cover the pot and roast in the oven until the duck is tender but not falling off the bone, about 1½ hours. Remove the duck from the fat and set aside.

Make the braised lamb shanks: Put all the ingredients in a medium saucepot; cover with water. Bring to a boil over high heat, then reduce to a simmer. Skim and discard any scum that rises to the surface. Simmer until the lamb is tender and breaking away from the bone, about 3 hours. Set aside.

Make the cassoulet: In a Dutch oven set over medium-high heat, heat the duck fat. Add the pork belly and cook until golden brown on all sides, about 3 minutes per side. Remove the pork belly and set aside, leaving the residual fat in the bottom of the pot.

Reduce the heat to medium. Add the celery, onion, carrot, leek, and garlic and cook until the onion is translucent and fragrant. Stir in the tomato

Recipe continues

3 cloves garlic, peeled and smashed

3 tablespoons tomato paste

4½ cups (945 g) dry navy beans, soaked overnight

1 bouquet garni (2 sprigs thyme, 2 sprigs rosemary, and a small bunch of flat-leaf parsley tied together with butcher's twine)

2 quarts (2 L) chicken stock

¼ cup (60 ml) canola oil

7 Toulouse sausages

Kosher salt

1½ cups (150 g) dry bread crumbs

paste and cook 2 minutes. Add the beans and return the pork belly to the pot. Immerse the bouquet garni in the beans and pour in the stock.

Increase the heat to high and bring to a boil, then immediately reduce to low. Simmer until the beans are just tender enough to squish between your fingers, about 1½ hours.

Preheat the oven to 400°F (205°C). In a medium cast-iron pan set over medium heat, heat the oil. Sear the sausages in batches until golden brown, about 3 minutes per side.

Discard the herb bundle from the Dutch oven. Pour the beans into a large baking dish.

Tear the meat from the lamb shank bones, chop into large chunks, and stir into the beans. Season with salt as needed.

Nestle the sausages into the bean mixture. Cover the beans and sausage with the bread crumbs. Arrange the duck confit on top. Bake in the oven until the duck is golden and crispy, about 25 minutes.

Blanquette Ris de Veau

SERVES: 4 SKINNY FRENCH
PEOPLE

PREP TIME: 1 DAY

FOR THE SWEETBREADS:

1 onion, peeled and quartered

1 carrot, peeled and cut into chunks

1 stalk celery, cut into chunks

2 bay leaves

1 tablespoon black peppercorns

A few sprigs thyme

A few sprigs parsley

Kosher salt

2 pounds (910 g) sweetbreads

FOR THE VEGETABLES:

2 tablespoons unsalted butter

6 cremini mushrooms, quartered

2 cups (480 ml) veal stock

2 carrots, peeled and cut into 2-inch- (5 cm) long pieces

15 pearl onions, peeled

Ingredients continue

Working in French restaurants, you learn to love offal. I didn't know what offal was as a kid, but I was the one at the kitchen counter waiting patiently for the roasted goose heart, duck livers, or chicken gizzards. I loved variety meats from a very young age. I was fascinated with the textures and flavors; it always tasted so good to me. I'd season the meats with some salt and ask my mom for more hearts. But I was always denied because there was only one heart per bird.

The first time I worked with sweetbreads was at Le Sélect. We served a lot of them, and this is one of my all-time favorite preparations. Sweetbreads are the gateway drug to offal. If you've ever eaten at a French bistro, you know what I mean. And if you don't know that the sweetbread is the thymus gland, which is the gland in the throat of the calf, then you should Google yourself some sweetbreads. Poached, pressed, peeled, and fried in brown butter, then placed in a pot of warm, creamy veal stock with carrots and onions from a white roux and finished with egg yolks whisked with crème fraîche, chopped parsley, a few cracks of pepper, and a big ol' squeeze of lemon. To this day, I love to eat this out of the pot with some crusty baguette.

I really hope you make this recipe and love it as much as I do. It's perfect for when there's snow on the ground and there's a fireplace crackling away. That sounds like something from a cookbook.

—

Prepare an ice bath.

Make the sweetbreads: We are going to make court bouillon. In a large pot set over high heat, bring 3 quarts (2.8 L) cold water to a boil. Add the onion, carrot, celery, bay leaves, peppercorns, thyme, and parsley; simmer 20 minutes. Add enough salt so it tastes like a seasoned soup.

Place the sweetbreads in the simmering court bouillon and cook 6 minutes, then place in the ice bath. Once the sweetbreads are cold, use a paring knife to peel off the lining and any connective tissue. Place the sweetbreads in a bowl and cover with a damp paper towel; cover again with plastic wrap, then refrigerate.

Make the vegetables: Set a large pan over medium heat and melt the butter. Brown the mushrooms, then add the veal stock, carrots, and onions cook 20 minutes. Set aside.

Make the blanquette (sauce): In a medium pot set over medium heat, melt the butter; when it's bubbling, add the flour and, using a wooden spoon, stir constantly until cooked, 10 minutes. You're making a blond roux—not golden brown. Add the veal stock; it will bubble. (I like to add just a little stock first and whisk the mixture, making sure to eliminate any lumps from

Recipe continues

1 cup (2 sticks/225 g) unsalted butter

½ cup (65 g) all-purpose flour

3 cups (720 ml) veal stock, plus more if needed

3 egg yolks

½ cup (120 ml) crème fraîche

2 tablespoons Dijon mustard

Pinch cloves

2 tablespoons parsley, chopped

1 tablespoon chervil, chopped

1 tablespoon tarragon, chopped

FOR THE LENTILS DU PUY:

2 tablespoons unsalted butter

2 tablespoons olive oil

1 onion, diced

1 carrot, peeled and diced

1 stalk celery, diced

1 leek, cleaned and diced

2 cloves garlic, peeled and smashed

2 cups (380 g) lentils

4 cups (960 ml) chicken stock

1 bay leaf

A few sprigs thyme

the roux. Then I whisk quickly and add the rest of the stock.) Bring to a boil; it will thicken. If it's too thick, add more stock. Turn the heat down to low and let it simmer gently, 5 minutes.

In a bowl, slowly whisk together the egg yolks, crème fraîche, and mustard; add the cloves. Carefully add a ladleful of the blanquette sauce in the mixture while whisking to temper. When combined, slowly pour this mixture into the pot of blanquette sauce while whisking.

Add the sweetbreads and the reserved mushrooms, carrots, and pearl onions to the sauce and warm everything nicely. Add the parsley, chervil, and tarragon.

Make the lentils du puy: In a medium pot set over medium heat, heat the butter and oil. Add the onion, carrot, celery, leek, and garlic and cook until tender, 8 minutes. Pour in the lentils and cover with the chicken stock, bay leaf, and thyme. Cook until the lentils are tender, 15 minutes; remove the bay leaf and thyme.

On a plate, serve the sweetbreads and vegetable mixture, with the lentils on the side.

Roasted Breast of Veal

—
SERVES: 6
PREP TIME: 5 HOURS
—

1 veal breast

3 tablespoons Dijon mustard

Good olive oil

Sea salt and freshly ground black pepper

8 Yukon gold potatoes, peeled and quartered

6 shallots, peeled

½ head white cabbage, quartered with core attached

1 bunch thyme, leaves picked

Good honey

1 (750 ml) bottle dry white wine

2 cups (4 sticks/455 g) unsalted butter

Juice of 1 lemon (optional)

Apple cider vinegar (optional)

Cooking simply is best. That will never change. It will never be out of style. It will always be cool. It will always taste better. This dish is inspired by my time in Paris. When I went, I was twenty-nine years old and there for only four days. I mostly ate at bistros, but my dinner at Le Baratin was my favorite: We had a dish of roasted veal breast that blew my mind. The whole experience was perfect, including the chalkboard menu brought tableside and read to you like a mother to a child. My wife and I asked if the chef could cook a few of her favorite dishes for us. After the raw mackerel with lardo and raspberry, the broth of pork bone and mascot grapes, the veal brains in butter sauce, and the perfectly cooked slices of potatoes, we received a roasted veal breast. It was light, it was fatty, and it was crunchy. It was perfection. It was magnificent. It was a dish that made me fall in love with France. I chewed the meat off the bones while the salty, garlicky fat dripped down my fingers, past my wrist, and down to my elbow before I licked it like a feral dog from the streets of Paris.

—

Preheat the oven to 250°F (120°C). Remove the veal from the refrigerator and let it come to room temperature, about 1 hour.

Rub the veal with the mustard and splash it with some oil; sprinkle salt and pepper all over the breast and bones. Place in a large deep roasting pan and roast in the oven 3 hours, letting the fats, silverskin, and tendons break down.

Meanwhile, in a large pot of salted boiling water, parcook the potatoes; once they become almost fork-tender, drain and place on a baking sheet to cool.

Remove the roasting pan from the oven. Place the potatoes, shallots, and cabbage under and around the veal and liberally drizzle with oil and season with more salt and pepper. Confetti the thyme leaves over the veal and veggies and drizzle the cabbage with honey. Continue to roast another 30 minutes to 1 hour, cranking the heat to 400°F (205°C) for the last ½ hour of cooking to get some char on the veal and the vegetables.

The veal will be cooked perfectly when it's not falling off the bone but you can push a butter knife through the widest part and it goes through without resistance. Remove the roasting pan from the oven; place the vegetables on a plate and put the veal on a cutting board. Cover both with aluminum foil and a kitchen towel for 30 minutes.

Recipe continues

Place the roasting pan on the stove over medium heat. Add the wine and stir, scraping up all the bits from the bottom of the pan with a wooden spoon. Next, add the butter and, with a kitchen towel wrapped round the handle, swirl the pan over the heat in a circular fashion, like a miner sifting for gold in the Klondike. This will give you a great little pan sauce. You can add some lemon juice or a splash of vinegar if necessary.

Carve the veal and place on a plate with the shallots, cabbage, and potatoes and top with some sauce.

Bouillabaisse

SERVES: 4 TO 6
PREP TIME: 3 HOURS

FOR THE FISH FUMET:

1 large grouper head

4 onions, peeled and quartered

1 carrot, peeled and quartered

1 stalk celery, quartered

½ bulb fennel, quartered

1 leek, cleaned and quartered

1 tablespoon white peppercorns

1 tablespoon fennel seed

1 tablespoon star anise

Rind of 1 orange

FOR THE ROUILLE:

3 cloves garlic, peeled

3 egg yolks

½ roasted red pepper, peeled and seeded

2 tablespoons Dijon mustard

4 tablespoons (60 ml) white wine vinegar

Few pistils saffron

1 tablespoon prepared horse-radish

2 cups (480 ml) canola oil

Zest of 1 lemon

Juice of ½ lemon

Kosher salt (optional)

Ingredients continue

Bouillabaisse is *the* fish soup. It was first made in Marseilles, France, from the fish that the fishermen couldn't sell. I learned this from Google. The bony rockfish was simmered in a bouillon with Pernod, tomato, and saffron. This is how we are going to make the dish in this book. This is not how we did it at Le Sélect. There, we made a tomato-and-anise broth with leeks, fennel, Pernod, and saffron and added in shrimp, scallops, a few mussels, clams, and whatever day-old fish we didn't sell the night before: turbot, monkfish, or sea bream. We would place all the seafood and fish into containers, and when we'd get an order, we would heat the broth, then add the fish and shellfish according to the proper cooking times. And we always garnished the soup with a buttery, crispy crouton and tangy rich rouille.

When *you* make this soup, you must find the best fish shop to get the best fish you can. Go a few days before you want to cook it and ask the person behind the counter what's coming in over the next week and see if you can get any special fish or seafood. Langoustines and red mullets will probably be difficult to find, but bouillabaisse can be made with so many different kinds of fish or shellfish, so I'd make this soup with whatever the fishmonger has that's freshest. Talk to him or her about cooking times—monkfish may take three to four minutes to cook off the bone, but a fillet of sea bream is much thinner and more delicate, so it takes only two to three minutes. Remember that building a relationship with your fishmongers and butchers is important because cooking great food always starts with your purveyors.

Make the fish fumet: Rinse the grouper head under cold running water, then split the head in half with a knife from the bottom of the head through the jaw. Discard the gills.

Place the head in a stockpot and fill with enough cold water to cover all the contents; bring to a boil, skim the scum that rises to the top, and turn down the heat to a low simmer.

Add the onions, carrot, celery, fennel, leek, peppercorns, fennel seed, star anise, and orange rind. Simmer 1 hour, and then turn off the heat and let the fumet steep 30 minutes.

Make the rouille: In the bowl of a food processor, place the garlic, egg yolks, roasted red pepper, mustard, vinegar, saffron, and horseradish; blend until fully incorporated and smooth. While food processor is running, slowly pour the oil in a thin, steady stream until it forms a beautiful rouille, like aïoli. Add the lemon zest and a little juice and some salt if needed.

Make the bouillabaisse broth and seafood: In a blender, place the onions, celery, fennel, leek, carrot, jalapeño, chiles, and garlic; add the oil and blend slowly until fully incorporated with the consistency of pulp.

Recipe continues

171

2 onions, peeled

1 stalk celery

1 bulb fennel

1 leek, cleaned

1 carrot, peeled

1 jalapeño pepper

2 red serrano chiles

1 head garlic, peeled

½ cup (120 ml) canola oil

2 tablespoons tomato paste

1 (6-ounce/170 g) can good
tomato puree

6 Yukon gold potatoes, peeled

1 cup (240 ml) Pernod

4 pistils saffron

Kosher salt

4 red mullets, skin on

½ pound (225 g) cod, cut into
2 to 3-ounce (55 to 85 g) pieces

½ pound (225 g) striped bass,
cut into 2 to 3-ounce (55 to
85 g) pieces

2 pounds (910 g) littleneck
clams

6 langoustines

8 large fresh scallops

6 jumbo shrimp

1 pound (455 g) mussels

FOR SERVING:

1 good baguette

Unsalted butter

Pour the blended mixture into a Dutch oven set over medium heat; cook until tender, golden brown, and caramelized, about 1 hour. Add the tomato paste and cook, stirring with a wooden spoon, 5 minutes. Add the tomato puree; cook 20 minutes. Add 1 gallon (3.8 L) of the fish fumet; bring to a boil and simmer 30 minutes. Add the potatoes and cook another 30 minutes, then add the Pernod and saffron. Season to taste with salt. It is now ready for the seafood.

The seafood cooks for different amounts of time, so first add the fish, which takes the longest to cook. Add the red mullets, cod, and striped bass and cook 5 minutes. Add the clams and cook about 5 minutes; add the langoustines and cook 4 minutes; add the scallops and jumbo shrimp and cook 3 minutes; then add the mussels and cook until they open (should be almost instantly).

Pull out the seafood and place on a large platter; serve the broth separate. Place a big bowl of the rouille on the table and serve with a toasted baguette and some butter.

Choucroute Garnie

SERVES: 8
PREP TIME: 5 HOURS

2 cups (480 ml) duck fat

2 cloves garlic, peeled and smashed

1 tablespoon juniper berries

5 yellow onions, thinly sliced

Kosher salt

1 quart (32 ounces) sauerkraut

1 (750 ml) bottle good Riesling wine

1 cup (240 ml) good gin

3 quarts (2.8 L) chicken stock

1 lightly smoked ham hock

2 pounds (910 g) pork belly, cut into 1 by 2-inch (2.5 by 5 cm) pieces

2 bay leaves

4 Strasbourg sausages

4 Montbéliard sausages

1 four-bone rack pork loin

6 Yukon gold potatoes, peeled and halved lengthwise

1 cup (2 sticks/225 g) unsalted butter, melted

1 handful chopped flat-leaf parsley

Dijon mustard, for serving

Cornichons, for serving

Every time I go back and eat at Le Sélect, I get this dish. Spring, summer, fall, winter—whatever the temperature—if I'm at Le Sélect, I'm ordering a choucroute. In this recipe, we simmer the pork belly in the kraut; it's so soft that it's like molten rubies of pig-skin meat and fat. The super-snappy skin of the Strasbourg sausage; the heavily spiced Montbéliard sausage; the little morsels of braised ham hocks; the sour, buttery cabbage braised with Riesling and Dijon mustard; the side of cornichon . . . these just bring this whole dish to your face.

As you can tell, I love this dish. I'm just sitting here in my freezing-cold office, writing this book. It makes me go insane thinking I could just go to Le Sélect and eat a choucroute right now.

Frédéric, the owner of Le Sélect, is from Alsace, France, where choucroute originated, so he was very controlling over the dish. He is a pretty intense, tall blond German French man who's very stern and did not mess around at all with his French bistro. And why should he? If someone plated that choucroute the wrong way, he would somehow know about it, and that cook would get spoken with!

—

In a large Dutch oven set over high heat, melt the duck fat.

Place the garlic and the juniper berries in the duck fat; cook until the garlic is lightly golden and the juniper berries are toasting nicely, 1 to 2 minutes. Add the onions and season with 2 big pinches of salt. Stir the onions and cook them down until they're translucent and lightly golden.

Add the sauerkraut, wine, gin, stock, ham hock, pork belly, and bay leaves; turn the heat down to medium-low and cover the pot. Cook 2½ to 3 hours, stirring every 30 minutes. In the last 30 minutes, place the sausages in the pot and cover.

Preheat the oven to 400°F (205°C). Season the pork loin with salt and score the skin with a clean box cutter or sharp knife all the way across, going from top to bottom. Place the pork loin on a rack set on a baking sheet and roast until a thermometer inserted into the center of the eye of the pork loin reaches 140°F (60°C), about 45 minutes. Remove from the oven and let rest, 10 minutes; slice ¼ inch (6mm) thick.

In a large pot of boiling water, cook the potatoes until almost fork-tender, then transfer them to a pan with the melted butter and parsley; season with salt and set aside.

Recipe continues

Remove the pork belly, sausages, and ham hock from the choucroute. Using tongs, shred the meat off the ham hock and chop the meat and pieces of tendon (if there are any) and return to the pot. Give the choucroute a good stir—but be gentle. Check for seasoning and add salt if needed.

Scoop the choucroute onto a large platter and decorate it with steamy roasted pork. Stack the sausages, the slices of unctuous pork belly, and the pork loin, then pile the butter-parsley–covered potatoes and serve with a big bowl of mustard and cornichons.

Bavette

SERVES: 1
PREP TIME: 15 MINUTES

Canola oil

1 (7-ounce/200 g) bavette

Kosher salt and freshly ground black pepper

1 tablespoon unsalted butter

1 shallot, peeled and diced

2 tablespoons green peppercorns

¼ cup (60 ml) brandy

½ cup (120 ml) demi-glace

1 tablespoon thyme leaves

¼ cup (60 ml) heavy cream

At the restaurant, we would grill and slice probably 150 to 200 portions of bavette throughout lunch and dinner service. When I worked the grill, I would keep an ice bucket underneath to plunge my hands into, so I could just use my hands on the grill without using tongs. At one time, I could be grilling twelve bavettes, a couple lamb racks, and venison chops, and a couple salmon fillets or trout on the fish side of the grill, which I kept so oiled that when you put a fish on it, the fillet would slide. That's when I knew I was the master of my domain.

Side note: There are many cuts that a butcher may call bavette: flank, flap, skirt, or even hanger. Have a conversation with your butcher to find out more on the bistro cut, aka bavette.

Set a cast-iron pan over medium-high heat and get it smoking a little. Pour just enough oil to cover the entire bottom of the pan. Season the steak with salt and pepper. Place the steak in the pan and let it get golden brown on one side, about 2 minutes, then flip it to the other side. Turn down the heat to low. Flip it back and forth, cooking 30 seconds on each side, at least six times total, then remove the steak to a plate lined with a paper towel.

In the same pan, add 2 tablespoons oil, the butter, and shallot and cook until translucent, about 3 minutes. Add the peppercorns and cook 30 seconds; deglaze with the brandy. Watch out: It will set ablaze. Add the demi-glace and let melt, then add the thyme leaves and cream. Reduce 1 minute.

Place the bavette on a plate and pour all the sauce over the steak until it pools the entire plate to the rim.

Venison Rack with Chocolate Demi-Glace

—

SERVES: 3
PREP TIME: 30 MINUTES

—

FOR THE VENISON:

1 venison rack

½ cup (120 ml) canola oil

Kosher salt and freshly ground black pepper

¼ cup (½ stick/55 g) unsalted butter

2 cloves garlic, peeled

1 bunch rosemary

1 bunch thyme

FOR THE SAUCE:

¼ cup (60 ml) red wine vinegar

¼ cup (50 g) granulated sugar

½ cup (120 ml) port

½ cup (120 ml) Madeira wine

1 teaspoon good ground espresso beans

1 cup (240 ml) demi-glace

2 ounces (50 g) bittersweet Baker's Chocolate

Freshly ground black pepper

Juice of 1 lemon (optional)

2 tablespoons cold unsalted butter, cubed

Viggo Mortensen, Ed Harris, and Maria Bello came into Le Sélect once for dinner. It was the first time I'd ever seen a celebrity in real life. I was so stoked to see Viggo; the *Lord of the Rings* films were out, and it was so fucking mental. They were shooting *A History of Violence*, which is a great movie. I forget what Ed and Maria ordered, but Viggo ordered a venison chop rare, which was my station and I knew I wouldn't screw it up. I'd do everything in my power to make Viggo's chop the best venison chop he'd ever eaten! I wondered if he'd ever had a venison chop, or if this was his first: Was I going to cook Viggo his very first venison chop?

I was so nervous. Our venison chop was so legendary—it was a twelve-ounce chop of the softest meat. We served it with a chocolate demi-glace.

It's so fucking funny that I was so shook from seeing celebrities; but I was fresh out of cooking school and it was a different time. It was the early 2000s, before social media, when movie stars and celebrities were still able to have secret lives.

I found the perfect chop, which I grilled so perfectly—it was the most perfect rack that has ever been cooked. I let it rest with a perfect slab of butter that would keep it moist and buttery and give it that edge that I knew Viggo would love. I cradled his chop like it was a newborn baby panda—this venison chop was going to save lives—and placed it on the plate next to the green beans and the potato dauphinoise. I watched it leave the kitchen like a father watching his son leave for college. I was so proud of myself. One minute later the server returned, saying the chop was overcooked. Viggo did not like the venison!

I overcooked a venison chop for Aragorn, the king of Gondor, the warrior who saved Middle-earth! I was a loser. I let down my chef, my team. I let my parents down, my grandparents, my great-great-grandparents. I let everyone down. I'm human garbage. My entire soul jumped into a garbage can, poured gasoline all over myself, and lit my body ablaze!

Then, I cooked his rack again perfectly rare like I didn't care and he loved it. Vigs, remember me?

—

Prepare the venison: A venison rack often has a little silverskin running down the loin that you can remove with a paring knife, leaving the loin of the rack bare. There is no fat on the venison rack, so it will cook rather quickly, and you don't want to cook it too aggressively. You should french the bones as well, cutting away any of the rib meat from between bones: Using the bones as your guide, slide your knife down the side of one bone and then along the top of the loin and up the other bone. Once you've removed all the rib meat from between the bones, scrape all the meat from around the bones. And letting your meat come to room temperature will allow it to cook much better.

Recipe continues

Preheat the oven to 350°F (175°C). In a cast-iron pan set over medium-high heat, heat the oil. Season the venison with salt and pepper, then place it loin-side down in the middle of the pan. Sear until it's golden brown, then flip the rack so the bones are against the side of the pan and sear the bottom. Then, using tongs, flip the venison on its side, holding it straight up, and sear both sides.

Place the venison on a baking sheet and roast in the oven 5 minutes; tent with aluminum foil and let rest 15 minutes.

Set the cast-iron pan over medium heat. Add the butter, garlic, rosemary, and thyme; let it get frothy. Return the venison to the pan, with the bones leaning against the edge. Tilt the pan so the butter pools; baste the venison 3 minutes with the frothy, garlicky herbed brown butter. Transfer the venison to a cutting board and pour the butter garlic goodness all over it.

Make the sauce: In the same pan, add the vinegar and sugar and deglaze, swirling with a wooden spoon. Let it start to caramelize and really bubble, then add the port, Madeira, and espresso grounds and reduce by half, 10 minutes. Add the demi-glace and the chocolate, swirling constantly, with the pan handle (wrapped in a kitchen towel) in one hand and the wooden spoon in the other. Remove the sauce from the heat and add some pepper and a squeeze of lemon juice, if needed. Carefully pour the sauce through a fine chinois into a saucepot. Stir in the butter until melted (the sauce should still be hot).

Slice the venison rack between the bones into perfect medium-rare chops. Pool the sauce on the bottom of a warm plate and place the venison chops on top.

Pot-au-Feu

SERVES: 5 TO 7

PREP TIME: GET READY,
THIS TAKES 5 DAYS

15 ounces (.5 L) warm water

Kosher salt and freshly ground black pepper

15 ounces (500 g) ice

½ pound (225 g) beef brisket

1 beef rib

1 veal shank

1 oxtail

1 ox tongue

4 (2-inch/5 cm) pieces bone marrow

1 bouquet garni (thyme, parsley, and tarragon tied together with butcher's twine)

4 yellow onions, peeled

4 carrots, peeled

½ head white cabbage, quartered

1 rutabaga, peeled and quartered

4 leeks, cleaned and cut in half lengthwise

4 Yukon gold potatoes, peeled

3 bay leaves

Olive oil

Good mustard, salsa verde (page 271), and bread, for serving

Boiled meats are great. And pot-au-feu is the king of boiled meats. If done well, this dish will change your life. It requires more time than most recipes, and patience is key. No one wants a fridge full of brining meats, but that's what this takes. The brine is very important; it changes a very simple dish into a tasty meal. Cook the meat, broth, and vegetables in one pot. It's the original "slow cooker" meal, but everything isn't just mashed together. The bone marrow adds just enough fat to the broth. This dish is great fresh out of the pot, and it's even better the next day.

—

To make a 10% salt brine, pour warm water into a small pan. Add 3 ounces (100 g) salt and bring to a boil over high heat. Cover and remove from the heat and let sit for 10 minutes. Put the ice in a bowl or a large measuring cup. Pour the brine over the ice and stir until dissolved. Allow brine to cool to room temperature.

Brine the brisket, rib, veal, oxtail, and tongue in a large pot 4 days in the refrigerator. After 2 days place the bone marrow in its own pot of unsalted water and refrigerate. Change the water every day until end of brining; this leeches the blood.

Place the brined meat in a large pot and cover with cold water. Bring it to a boil, then pour the water down the sink. Place the meat back in the pot and add cold water; bring to a boil again, then turn down the heat to low. Skim the scum that rises to the top. Add the bone marrow and the bouquet garni to the pot; cover and cook 4 hours.

Add the onions, carrots, cabbage, rutabaga, leeks, potatoes, and bay leaves; simmer 1½ hours. Remove the vegetables and place on a platter; drizzle with some nice olive oil and sprinkle with salt and pepper.

Place the meat on a giant cutting board or platter. Peel and slice the tongue, slice the brisket and rib, and pull apart the rest of the meat with tongs. Ladle some of the broth into a big bowl. Put everything on a table with a bowl of good mustard, salsa verde, and lots of bread. Let everyone dig in!

La Palette

Twenty-four years old on the patio of Ronnie's—my favorite bar of all time.
I miss you so much. Damn you, sobriety.

Top left: Andrew and Jennifer
Top right: Shamez
Bottom left: The new La Palette
Bottom right: Melissa and Jennifer

TRY NOT TO BURN YOUR
RESTAURANT DOWN

I took a $10-per-hour pay cut to work at La Palette. That's how badly I wanted to work there. It was a ragtag team with only three cooks on weekends and two during the week, and if you were lucky you had one dishwasher during your shift who was typically one of your buddies doing it for beer money. This cook named Ben was supposed to show me the ropes. He asked me if I knew how to make soup. I asked him what kind of soup. He told me that they needed a soup of the day, so any kind. I know how to make soup, you fucking idiot. I just spent the last three years of my life working at one of the best French restaurants in Canada, you hippie fucking loser.

Mike Harrington, one of the chefs at Le Sélect, and Shamez Amlani, one of the bar managers, both left Le Sélect to open La Palette before I started. All I heard about them is that they opened up this bohemian, punk, magical bistro in Kensington Market. One story was that they had in the vast, deep, dark belly of Le Select, in the wine cellar, a cigar box full of magic mushrooms that they would dose each other with constantly. I always tried to look for it when I was working or to see if they forgot about a few of them. Who knows if it was true. All I knew is that I wanted to work for these guys one day.

Unfortunately, Mike left before I started there to open La Palette in Mexico—a bed and breakfast. I didn't meet him until my last year at the restaurant. During my time at La Palette, Shamez was my boss. He was emotional in the best and worst ways. He loved you, and he would take care of you, shower you in absinthe and vintage punk records; then he would verbally assault you if you ran out of one single slice of Morbier for the cheese plate.

Shamez stood up for himself and what he believed in. Before bike lanes were a civic issue, he and his merry men and women would be out on the streets, in ski masks, spray painting bike lanes around downtown Toronto and trying to get the lanes officially adopted. He started what became Pedestrian Sundays in Kensington Market. I enjoyed working for him. Every year Shamez would get a car from the dump, paint it white, leave it in front of the restaurant for a week for the neighbors and anyone visiting Kensington Market to sign, and then march it to the front of city hall as an act of protest. One time, when we were drunk and in the restaurant's patio late at night, Shamez pulled up in the annual car and stood on the hood, yelling about how much he hated them. Shamez was an anti-car man. My buddies and I ran up to the car and started hitting it. I punched through the window and blood started squirting out of my forearm. I went to the basement of La Palette, pulled out as much glass as I could, and taped it up with duct tape. I think that was on Trish's birthday. I love you, Trish.

I got to meet so many great people: Maria, Jennifer Castle, Dave Clark, Andrew Artedio, Lenny Miller, Kungfu, Kelsey, Michael J., Brook, Shelly, Joe, Missy, and Sam Higgs, aka Mudman—a tree-hugging, white Rasta guy who really is the best even though he has dreads.

At La Palette, we were allowed to have drinks but had to keep a tab on a piece of paper behind the bar. Many times I would work two weeks and end up owing more than my paycheck. On Saturday nights we would hang out at the restaurant after service and party until four or five in the morning, get a few hours of sleep, and then come back in for brunch at eight. Service started at ten. We would finish the last orders at three in the afternoon, wrap up our stations by 3:30, and then get annihilated on the patio. Summertime was the greatest thing.

One time me, Kungfu, and Lenny were drunk on the patio drinking fruli beer. We were all annihilated. The cooks for the Sunday night service came in and started cooking. All of a sudden they came out to have a cigarette. What we didn't know was that this fucking idiot cook, Kevin, put on a pot of duck confit and it overflowed and caught on fire.

A friendly neighbor ran across the street and told us, "Your chimney is on fire." We ran into the kitchen and saw a flaming pot of duck confit. We tried everything: We threw a bag of flour on it. We turned the gas off. We poured boxes of salt to try to extinguish the flames. Nothing worked. While we were inside trying to put it out, Shamez grabbed our only fire extinguisher and somehow got onto the roof without a ladder and sprayed down the chimney with all his might.

Nothing was working. We had to get this flaming pot of duck fat off the stove. As a last effort I wrapped kitchen towels around my arms and picked up the flaming sixteen-liter pot that held fifty duck legs with fat. Luckily I didn't burn myself because I'm so stealthy—or maybe it was the luck of a day-drunk cook.

I ended up working at La Palette for about two years, until my mind was crushed and my body was broken. What I learned there was that a restaurant is a real living organism of the people working in it. La Palette was high octane: It was a live wire of drugs, emotions, and alcohol. Plus Artedio, the most legendary server of all time, was notorious for leaving mid-service to grab a bag of coke or heroin because he claimed it was the only way to treat his hemorrhoids. And he had on his forearm a classic Snoopy tattoo with the phrase "stay positive" beneath. Needless to say it was time to move on.

Venison Tartare with Warm Bone Marrow Drippings

SERVES: 6
PREP TIME: 1½ HOURS

4 (2-inch/5 cm) pieces bone marrow

1 sprig rosemary

2 cloves garlic, peeled

1 pound (455 g) venison tenderloin

2 tablespoons peeled and finely diced shallots

2 egg yolks

1 tablespoon Dijon mustard, plus more as needed

Tabasco sauce

Zest and juice of 1 lemon

1 handful chopped flat-leaf parsley

Good olive oil

Kosher salt

1 loaf good sourdough bread, sliced

Cornichons, for serving (optional)

Raw venison tenderloin tossed simply with Dijon mustard, shallots, good olive oil, the zest and juice of a lemon, a few cracks of black peppercorns, and some really good sea salt. Then cover that mound of venison tartare with warm buttery bone marrow drippings.

At La Palette we served horse tartare. People would come for this dish like fiending crackheads to their dealers. Once customers tasted that raw horse, they went mad for it. I know eating horse is controversial. People fear what they don't understand. These beautiful, smart, strong animals are often raised for the purpose of eating, much like beloved cows, pigs, lamb, rabbits, goats, chickens, turkeys, quails, trout, deer, wild boar . . .

There are so many variations of tartare, and everyone has their favorite. I like mine simple, so the meat can shine.

—

Preheat the oven to 350°F (175°C). In an oven-safe pan, roast the bone marrow until the fat is fully rendered, 15 minutes. Add the rosemary and garlic and roast 20 more minutes. Remove the pan from the oven and pour the warm marrow fat into a small saucepan; reserve. Discard the bones.

Cut the tenderloin into thin slices against the grain, then pile it together. You should slice the meat and make little stacks of 5 slices. You should have 6 piles; each pile is a portion. Line up these little stacks on your cutting board. Then julienne those stacks and dice. Place the meat on a paper towel–lined plate and place in the fridge, uncovered, for up to 1 hour. In the meantime, prepare the rest of the recipe.

Remove the meat from the fridge and place in a bowl. Add the shallots, egg yolks, mustard, 7 splashes of Tabasco, lemon zest, half the lemon juice, and the parsley. Now drizzle enough olive oil to make it look like a glistening Arctic glacier. It shouldn't be swimming in oil, but it should be enough to make it loose and yet still together. It should have the consistency of an oozing, warm egg yolk. Gently stir until combined but not mashed. Keep the meat moving, using your spoon to dig into the yolks, breaking them into an oozy mess that coats the meat. Keep stirring until it becomes one mass; taste. Add salt if needed; if it needs acid, add more lemon juice; if it needs tang, add more mustard.

Grill the bread and season with salt. (Charred bread is best for venison tartare.) Spoon the tartare on the bread and cover it with the warm, buttery bone marrow drippings. Serve with a cornichon, if you feel like it. Enjoy this beautiful meat the way it should be: raw!

Snails on Toast

SERVES: 4 TO 6
PREP TIME: 30 MINUTES

2 (125 g) cans Escal Burgundy snails

¼ cup (60 ml) canola oil

6 tablespoons (85 g) unsalted butter

3 shallots, peeled and diced

1 carrot, peeled and diced

½ bulb fennel, trimmed and diced

1 stalk celery, diced

6 cremini mushrooms, caps diced and stems sliced

2 cloves garlic, peeled and minced

1 tablespoon tomato paste

1 cup (240 ml) Madeira wine

1 cup (240 ml) dry red wine

1 bay leaf

4 sprigs thyme

1 bunch tarragon, chopped

1 bunch parsley, chopped

1 bunch chervil, chopped

1 baguette, split and cut into 6-inch (15 cm) slices

We used canned snails from Burgundy for this dish at La Palette. I had never even seen real snails until I went to Paris for the first time. I love canned, but there's just something about fresh grilled snails with popping butter and good bread. The first time I made this at the restaurant I used cooking wine, which was pretty shit and super salty. It really fucked up the dish. I hate cooking wine: It's one of the worst things about restaurant cooking. By the time you reduce cooking wine, it would be super salty, so you would have to add so much acid that would fuck up this dish. Anyway, we would braise the snails for twenty to forty minutes, then pour them onto a baking sheet with cooked-down mirepoix and reduced wine, then, once cooled, place them in deli containers. When an order came in, we would place five snails with some of the reduced wine and mirepoix into one of those ceramic escargot dishes, place some roasted cremini mushroom caps on top, and pour a little clarified butter over it. Then we'd put it in the oven until it was popping and spitting all over the place. We would serve it with a weird roasted red pepper–feta relish with a chiffonade of basil. I'm not sure if that's fusion, but it was a fucking weird time in 2005. The following recipe is different from what I just talked about; no disrespect to the red pepper relish, but we're just gonna make snails on toast.

—

Rinse the snails under cold running water for 1 minute. They will smell like farts and grass, I find, which is a kinda chill smell.

Set a heavy medium saucepan over medium heat. Pour in the oil and add 2 tablespoons butter. Add the shallots, carrot, fennel, celery, mushrooms, and garlic and cook until translucent, 5 to 10 minutes.

Stir in the tomato paste and cook for a few minutes. Add the snails, the Madeira wine, red wine, bay leaf, and thyme. (Tie the thyme sprigs together with twine so you can pull them out easily after braising.) Bring to a boil, then turn down the heat and cook until the sauce is reduced by half, 10 to 15 minutes. Remove from the heat. Add 3 tablespoons butter and toss in a handful of the tarragon, parsley, and chervil.

Set a cast-iron pan over medium heat. Butter the bread slices and toast in the pan until golden brown on each side.

Spoon the snails over the bread, letting the sauce pool and fall over the sides. Enjoy!

Seared Foie Gras with Rice Pudding and Warm Date Marmalade

—
SERVES: 8
PREP TIME: 45 MINUTES
—

FOR THE FOIE GRAS:

1 whole lobe foie gras, cut into 1½ inch- (4 cm) thick slices

Kosher salt and freshly ground black pepper

FOR THE RICE PUDDING:

1 cup (200 g) short-grain white rice

1 tablespoon unsalted butter

1 teaspoon kosher salt

1 cup (240 ml) milk

1 cup (240 ml) heavy cream

½ cup (110 g) packed brown sugar

½ cup (120 ml) marshmallow fluff

FOR THE DATE MARMALADE:

1 tablespoon unsalted butter

½ teaspoon ground cloves

½ teaspoon ground allspice

½ teaspoon ground cardamom

12 whole Medjool dates, pitted

¼ cup (60 ml) apple cider vinegar

1 cup (240 ml) Madeira wine

Juice and zest of 1 lemon

Ingredients continue

This is the ultimate winter meal, or eat it whenever the fuck you want to. I love savory, sweet, and fatty. I love foie gras. I love rice pudding. I love dates. This dish is inspired by my time at La Palette. We could get away with serving foie gras with anything we liked. Put that fatty mouthwatering slab of duck liver on a dirty-water hot dog, and I'd still eat it. This dish has a warm-on-warm-on-warm mouthfeel. It tastes like a dream of you birthing yourself into a warm bath of maple syrup filled with thousands of little mermaids kissing your body at once. Well, that is what this dish does for me. Make sure you buy foie gras from a trusted butcher and that it's the highest grade.

—

Cook the foie gras: I don't like scoring foie gras before I sear it, but you can crosshatch the top and bottom if you'd like. Season the slices with salt and pepper. In a dry medium pan set over medium-high heat, place your foie gras a few slices at a time; do not overcrowd the pan. The foie gras will smoke and start rendering fat very quickly, so please don't turn your back on it. Once it is a golden dark brown, flip it. The edges should be nice and crispy on both sides, and the centers should have the consistency of melting butter. Remove to a paper towel–lined plate and repeat with the remaining foie gras. Let it rest as you would steak, poultry, pork, or any meat.

Make the rice pudding: Rinse the rice under cold running water. In a medium pot, combine 1½ cups (360 ml) cold water, the butter, salt, and rice; bring to a boil. Cover the pot and turn the heat down to low; cook 10 minutes, then remove from the heat and let sit 10 minutes.

In another medium pot set over medium heat, place the milk, cream, and brown sugar; cook 8 minutes, reducing the liquid by half. Add the cooked rice and stir until nice and creamy. Add the marshmallow fluff, which is what puts this rice pudding over the top. Stir it in only a little—don't fully incorporate the fluff so you can have these little marshmallow pockets, which are ridiculous!

Make the date marmalade: In a medium pot set over medium heat, melt the butter, then add the cloves, allspice, and cardamom. Cook for just a minute to open all the flavors, then add half the dates. (I leave them whole so they have more texture when they break down.) Add the vinegar; let it

Recipe continues

1 cup (240 ml) good maple syrup

1 tablespoon ground cinnamon

Freshly ground black pepper

reduce 1 minute. Add the wine and lemon juice. Cook 15 minutes over low heat and let it turn into a beautiful sticky marmalade. Add the remaining dates and just a little water if the marmalade becomes too tight. Then right at the last moment, add the lemon zest.

To serve: In a small pot set over medium heat, warm the maple syrup (don't bring it to a boil). I hate when people serve room-temperature syrup—it should always be warm. Spoon some rice pudding into a bowl, add a few tablespoons of date marmalade, and top with a slice of seared foie gras. Pour 2 tablespoons maple syrup over it, and sprinkle with a dusting of cinnamon and a few cracks of pepper. Trust me on this!

Quack and Track: Duck Confit and Beef Tenderloin

—

SERVES: 4 TO 6

PREP TIME: 2 DAYS PLUS
3 HOURS

—

FOR THE DUCK CONFIT:

½ cup (125 g) kosher salt

1 cup (200 g) granulated sugar

Zest of 1 orange

8 cloves garlic, peeled

½ bunch flat-leaf parsley

½ bunch thyme, leaves picked

4 duck legs

4 cups (1 L) duck fat

FOR THE BEEF TENDERLOIN:

2 pounds (910 g) beef tenderloin

Canola oil

Kosher salt

A few sprigs thyme

A few sprigs rosemary

2 cloves garlic, crushed

3 tablespoons unsalted butter

FOR THE BLACKBERRY DEMI-GLACE:

1 shallot, peeled and minced

1 tablespoon unsalted butter

2 ounces (60 ml) sherry

2 tablespoons blackberry jam

1 cup (240 g) demi-glace

1 pint (280 g) blackberries, chopped

Freshly ground black pepper

1 lemon

Unsalted butter (optional)

La Palette was the first restaurant in Toronto to serve horse. This came with controversy and responsibility. We often had protests out front because of this. Shamez Amlani, the co-owner, loved when the protesters came. We would offer them tea and even sometimes a plate of sliced horse tenderloin, upsetting the protesters even more. Horse is a type of meat that can easily be questioned: Where does it come from? Are you eating an old racehorse, an old farm horse, or a horse that was put down for a broken leg? Our horse came from a farm in Quebec; they were slaughtered in Indiana and then brought back to Quebec for consumption.

The French and Italians have been eating horse for centuries. And it is worth every bite. I'm a firm believer in, if you eat meat, why not all meat? The flavor is right between venison and beef—sweeter than beef and softer than venison. Shamez named this dish "Quack and Track" to draw attention, and it is still on the menu some seventeen years later. For my version I paired sweet and crispy duck confit with juicy rich beef for an amazing yet nonsensical pairing. I always said that people had to have La Palette's version if it was their first time at the restaurant. It is so iconic. It is so good. We served it with a jam demi-glace made with Bonne Maman blackberry preserves, potato gratin, and seasonal vegetables.

I would often watch from the kitchen when I knew someone was trying horse for the first time. If people braved through all the smoke and mirrors and dug into this ruby of precious meat, they were in for a meal of a lifetime. One bite, and they would be hooked. People would often come back within the week for a second helping. Working at La Palette made me think outside the box—cooking French food and the way I lived my life. It had a huge impact on how I cooked at my future restaurants. Fuck the rules and what people think.

—

Make the duck confit: In a blender, combine the salt, sugar, orange zest, garlic, parsley, and thyme leaves; blend until the mixture turns bright green and is fully incorporated.

Trim any loose skin from the duck legs with a paring knife; the skin should just cover the flesh. Place the legs flesh side up, skin side down in a glass casserole dish and rub the salt-sugar cure completely over the legs. Cover with plastic wrap and place in the fridge 24 hours.

Rinse the duck legs in a sink over a colander to catch all the herbs (so you don't mess up your plumbing). Pat the duck legs as dry as you can.

Preheat the oven to 250°F (120°C). In a heavy-bottomed enameled Dutch oven over medium heat, warm the duck fat until it is a yellowish gold liquid. Place the duck legs in the pot and completely submerge them in the liquid. Cover and roast in the oven 2 hours.

Recipe continues

Remove from the oven and let stand until the duck legs are at room temperature. In a smaller oven-safe dish, line up the duck legs in two rows, with the legs up. Pour enough duck fat over them to cover the meat, then place in the refrigerator 24 hours. Setting the duck legs for this amount of time makes such a difference in taste and texture.

Make the beef tenderloin: Cut the tenderloin into 6 medallions, about 5-ounce (140 g) each. In a medium cast-iron pan over medium-high heat, pour ¼ inch (6 mm) of oil, completely covering the pan to allow for even browning. Season the steaks with salt. Lightly sear the steaks three at a time so you don't overcrowd the pan. You don't want a hard sear; you want a light sear. You want to roll the meat around like a baby bear rolling a groundhog. Add 2 tablespoons butter and paddle the meat from side to side, top to tail.

Add the thyme, rosemary, garlic, and butter. It will froth and bubble. Place 3 of the steaks at the ten o'clock position in the pan and leave enough space for the butter to flow over the steaks while you baste them using a spoon. Cook 5 to 6 minutes and baste about 1 minute per side; place the steaks on a plate and let them rest. Repeat with the remaining steaks; pour the warm herbed butter over all the steaks.

Make the blackberry demi-glace: In a medium saucepan set over low heat, sauté the shallot in the butter until translucent. Next, add the sherry, black-berry jam, demi-glace, and blackberries. (You don't want to burn or reduce it any further.) Add a few cracks of pepper and a squeeze of lemon juice. You could add a knob of butter to round it out.

Serve with your favorite starch and vegetables.

NOAH'S ARK:
THE INFAMOUS MIXED GRILL

This was the biggest headache ever and that's why I'm not going to write this recipe. We had the smallest 12-inch- (30.5 cm) wide half-broken grill at La Palette, and we grilled all our meats for the mixed grill. We had elk long loin, horse tenderloin, wild boar tenderloin, caribou tip meat, ostrich loin, venison back strap, musk ox, water buffalo strip, bison flank, lamb rack, rabbit loin, and sometimes moose.

We would make 2 to 3-ounce (55 to 80 g) medallions of the meat, chops of the lamb, and chops of the wild boar. We had a list of all the meats on the menu, and you could pick three from the mix, or all of them if you wanted to be a savage. Shamez Amlani, the restaurant's co-owner, would love to push people into getting Noah's Ark, the infamous platter of all the grilled meats. So just think for a second: We had this great little bistro that had about forty-five seats inside and fifteen seats on the patio, and a small broken grill. Imagine getting an order that looked like this: 2 steak frites, 1 horse tenderloin, 1 cassoulet, 1 bouillabaisse, and 3 mixed grills.

At La Palette we had only one cook making all the mains, one or two doing cold appetizers and dessert, and hopefully a dishwasher on Friday and Saturday nights. Now, we didn't have fridges in the hot section, so every time we got an order, we had to memorize two or three orders at a time and run around the corner to the sunken walk-in refrigerator (yes, the walk-in was sinking into the Kensington Market earth). We'd grab all the proteins out of the fridge, then run back and place them on the seasoning trays, organize the pans, brush the grill, and start cooking. We'd throw the cassoulet into a pan, the duck confit into the oven, and start warming the broth for the bouillabaisse, making sure to leave the fish and shellfish in the walk-in until the last second. We'd start grilling the steaks for the steak frites, and once they came off, we would line up the proteins for the mixed grill, so that we wouldn't mess up the order. Then we'd gather all the starches and sides and veggies. It was a nonstop dance and shuffle like no place I'd worked before or after—it was complete chaos every single day and night! But it worked. We would go to the market each day and buy fresh seasonal veggies like asparagus, bok choy, garlic scapes, pattypan squash, runner beans, green beans, and fresh tomatoes. Potts—an eccentric, classic Toronto vegetable vendor—has the best produce in the market! It was the only place that actually used farmers. People won't want to hear this, but every single market buys all the same imported produce from the Ontario Food Terminal. Potts would work directly with all the best farmers, which made it easy to get great vegetables that we could usually just pan-fry quickly with some lemon juice, olive oil, garlic, and salt and pepper just to keep our heads above water.

Anyway, most important, we had better not have overcooked or undercooked the mixed grill, because if Shamez picked up the plates and then walked back to the kitchen with crazy eyes, we knew something went wrong, and that's when the wheels would come off! He would lose his cool and call us all kinds of names! He loved to call me a fat cokehead, but I really didn't care because I drank pretty much for free, and I *was* a fat cokehead, so that was a smart diss, Sham! Someone ordered the wild boar, medium, and the ostrich, rare, so why the fuck is the bison medium-well? He'd say, WTF happened, and then I'd say I don't know, I cooked what was in the chit, man! And then we would have to re-fire that person's mixed grill or try to save it by cooking the undercooked piece again or re-cooking a fresh piece to replace an overcooked piece. It was so fucking rat-fucked. All this shit happened three or four times a night. It was confusing to begin with—like why the fuck would anyone want to eat twelve different meats at once, and why the fuck wouldn't we have a proper grill that could cook meat properly? Holy fucking fuck, this place broke my brain.

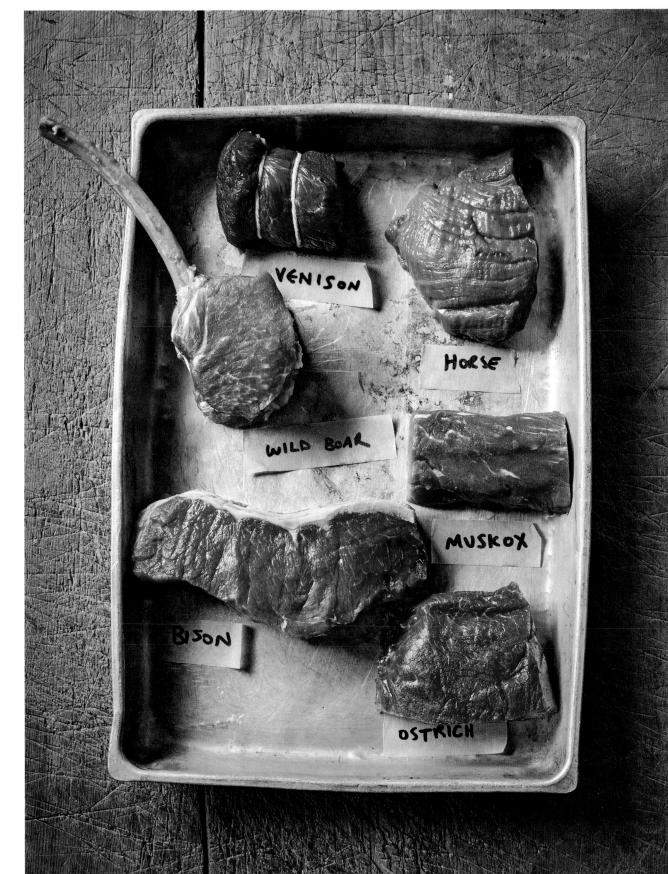

CHAPTER 8

Castor Design

Castor is French for "beaver."

Top left: Kei
Top right: Brian
Bottom left and right: Castor Design studio

PI IS EXACTLY 3

What the fuck is Castor Design? Let me tell you. Castor Design is a Toronto-based design studio run by Brian Richer and Kei Ng, who I truly love. Without their patience and trust I would not be who I am today, as a chef or as a man. What I've learned from them about restraint, design, architecture, business, music, and life can never be repaid. Brian is a stone carver, Renaissance-man artist, and Kei is an architect by trade who does phenomenal leatherwork and is an unbelievable chef in his own right. He is the surrogate dad I never made happy (but I had a real dad who *was* proud of me, so having a boss who didn't seem to like me right away was weird and uncomfortable for me). I got a phone call from the legendary Chris Taylor Wright, a waiter at Le Sélect who was a Samuel Beckett–type character. He asked if I wanted to open a restaurant with Brian Richer. "Who the fuck is that?" I asked. Chris told me that he went to university with Brian, who used to read Nietzsche by candlelight, wrapped in a blanket, smoking cigs. I said, "That's a vibe." At that point, I was pretty overworked at La Palette. Fuck it, I could open a restaurant and be the real chef, finally, I thought. It was an opportunity to make my own menu from the ground up. It would be my restaurant. Chris said if I was down he would set up an interview. He called me back in five minutes. "Can you go meet him now?" he asked. They were at the space working, which meant that they were smoking cigs and listening to Hüsker Dü. And that's how Oddfellows got started.

Oddfellows

*Broke my teeth when my pedal broke and I flipped over the handlebars
riding my bicycle home from Oddfellows. I was twenty-six at the time.
I'm really happy my father-in-law is a dentist.*

Oddfellows was beautifully fucked up.

THE CENTER WILL NOT HOLD

Brian and Kei always had crazy ideas. Buying a 1973 Winnebago Indian that barely ran could have been the best idea they ever had. They got this fucking thing for like $3,000. Brian and Kei turned it into a faux-fur-covered interior with a wood-burning oven that we had in a parking space behind the restaurant. It served as a private dining room where we only played Neil Young. And someone stole my records; if you find them or you have them, please return them to me. Soon word spread and people would call the restaurant and ask, "I heard you have a Winnebago where there are no rules. Can I rent it for my bachelor party?" And we would say, "Of course!" We thought we were killing it because we would charge them $100 on top of their food and beverages.

Another crazy idea was our Grazing Nights. Every Sunday we would charge $15 for an all-you-can-eat buffet, unless you were our friend, which meant it was free food and, most of the time, beer. It was the opposite of every buffet you have ever experienced. We would fill our twenty-six-foot-long marble table entirely with food. It started with charcuterie, which we bought from stores—thousands of dollars of prosciutto legs, cheese, and bread. Next, we did two twenty-six-foot-long subs. A bakery in Kensington Market made eight-foot-long sub rolls that we connected and filled with charcuterie that cost, all together, $3,000. I remember forty people showing up (half of whom were our friends so they ate for free). Who wouldn't want to go to a restaurant and slam one of our famous cocktails—called Death Mule—and eat a fucking one-foot slice of sub? Or how about summertime Taco Hell, years before Toronto's epic taco fad, where we had all-you-can-eat bowls of salsas, stewed meats, and freshly made tortillas? Imagine a world where there is free, unlimited guacamole. It would be a street party where there would be sixty kids outside on the street drinking beers and eating tacos. We were never busted by the cops. In the winter, we settled into Pierogi Night in Canada, where we would play old VHS tapes of the Summit Series—a series of hockey games between Canada and the USSR in 1972—on loop. The table would be filled with fried and boiled potato, cheese, pork and potato, and beef and potato pierogis complete with green onions, sour cream, applesauce, and caramelized onions. I loved Pierogi Night because our dishwasher, and my hero, Jesse B. Harris would boil and fry all the pierogis while I took part in the festivities by doing everything I could get my little hands on. Nose beers, wink.

Grazing Nights is one of the main reasons why Oddfellows no longer exists. We lost so much money on them. I'll just say that we were ahead of our time. Every Toronto restaurant or bar that seats fewer than sixty ripped our vibe, even if they didn't realize it. We were the first hipster restaurant, in the truest sense. Young punks serving great food (sometimes) and shitty cocktails, and trying our best to provide hospitality in our unique way, not turning down the music for anyone, and having the best time of our lives. People were at the house party that we had five nights a week in this very small, special space that we happened to call Oddfellows.

We were ten years too early (due to our lack of experience), but that's one of the things I love about restaurants. Brian and I talk about what would happen if we reopened Oddfellows. We know how to run restaurants now: We understand real food costs, inventory, labor costs, and that you don't have to give every person you know free beer all night, every night. We understand that you don't have to listen to Hüsker Dü, the Replacements, or Cro-Mags at full volume at 6 P.M., when you first open your doors. We understand that doing coke most nights of the week doesn't make you work harder.

We had a great, all-star-level team at Oddfellows: Mattitude, Jenny Orenda, Allison, Bloody, Millman, Grandma, Vrooman-Captain Buzzkill, Shelly, Joe, Streets, Jesse B. Harris, and Dark Darrell. I knew that Kei—who we called the Dark Overlord—was often cold, but he cared very much about us and deep down loved us very much. He was the serious one. I've always been in awe of both Kei and Brian. The most important things I learned from them are restraint and when to stop. Without both friends I wouldn't have my appreciation for design.

"Fake it till you make it" is a great saying, but if you never make it, you'd better have enough common sense to shut it down. Playing restaurant is one thing, but destroying a restaurant because of your stupidity, ego, and heavy drug use is another. Oddfellows closed in two years. When I think back about my time there, I always wonder how I didn't get fired. We'll have our memories, forever. RIP Oddies.

Top left and bottom right: The Winnebago that changed the world
Top right (left to right): Brian, me, Jesse, and McLeod hanging in the Winnebago
Bottom left: We traded Vice a Christmas party for a full-page ad in the print magazine. It was a photograph of this tattoo on my butt advertising the restaurant. I don't know if it was smart or not, but our restaurant is now closed. Some would say I'm a genius, some would say I'm an idiot. I've had a lot of mistakes to learn from.

Stew for Two

SERVES: 8

PREP TIME: 4 HOURS
PLUS 1 DAY

FOR THE STEW:

1 deboned venison shoulder, cut
into 1-inch (2.5 cm) cubes

1 deboned leg of lamb, cut into
1-inch (2.5 cm) cubes

6 deboned beef ribs, cut into
1-inch (2.5 cm) cubes

2 pounds (910 g) pork belly, cut
into 1-inch (2.5 cm) cubes

Kosher salt and freshly ground
black pepper

All-purpose flour

Canola oil

4 onions, diced

1 leek, cleaned and diced

2 pounds (910 g) cremini
mushrooms, chopped

2 stalks celery, chopped

2 carrots, peeled and chopped

2 parsnips, peeled and chopped

1 celery root, peeled and
chopped

1 rutabaga, peeled and chopped

4 tablespoons (65 g) tomato
paste

8 cups (2 L) red wine

8 cups (2 L) beef stock

½ bunch thyme, leaves picked
and chopped

1 bay leaf

½ bunch parsley, chopped

Ingredients continue

I know it says "for two," but I'm assuming you are a popular person who needs to cook for lots of cool people.

I think this dish is the reason Brian Richer and Kei Ng wanted to open Oddfellows. They were obsessed with using pressure cookers. Opening and releasing the pressure at the table in front of guests with the incredible aroma . . . I was left with the job of making this dream come true. Brian and Kei sourced the small individual pressure cookers in Little India on Toronto's east side. We would make a stew with venison, beef short rib, and lamb, potatoes, rutabaga, and parsnips. This was a very hearty stew: If the world ended, this would be the stew you needed to fight off an army of zombie werewolves. We would make large batches of the stew, and then when an order came in, we would fill a small pressure cooker halfway with cold stew and a little beef stock, then warm it with the lid off. On pickup we would add butter, lots of thyme, sliced green onions, a little more seasoning, if needed, and a little shot of lemon juice to really balance it out. Then we would place the top on and pressurize the stew. It would take only a few moments.

Then we would give this meat bomb to our brave servers and even braver customers. We would stop everything in the kitchen to watch every time to make sure it didn't explode. You would have to let that steam fly out of the little chimney, or it would completely explode. The moment the server opened it and there was no explosion, we would go back to work. We had only one explosion over two years—our manager at the time released it seconds too early, and hot, bubbling stew flew everywhere. Luckily, no one was really burned, but it was scary and we learned our lesson.

We loved the smell of the stew filling our small restaurant. (We hoped everyone would order it!) We would serve the stew with grilled sourdough bread and honey butter, horseradish bacon-creamed fingerling smashed potatoes, and a bunch of roasted vegetables. This is how you make stew!

Make the stew: Season the venison, lamb, beef, and pork with salt and pepper and dust with flour. Set a large Dutch oven over medium-high heat and pour 1 inch (2.5 cm) of oil. Sear the meat in batches, then place on a baking sheet. Take your time and make sure the meat is browned evenly and the flour doesn't burn, about 4 minutes per side.

Preheat the oven to 300°F (150°C). Pour out half the oil, then add the onions, leek, mushrooms, celery, carrots, parsnips, celery root, and rutabaga and cook until sweated, about 10 minutes. Add the tomato paste and stir into the vegetables. Add all the meat back to the pot and pour in the red wine and stock; stir with a wooden spoon and scrape the bottom of the pot, then add the thyme, bay leaf, and parsley.

Recipe continues

2 pounds (910 g) fingerling
potatoes

Kosher salt and freshly ground
black pepper

½ pound (225 g) slab bacon,
sliced into lardons

2 tablespoons prepared horseradish

1 cup (240 ml) heavy cream

1 bunch green onions, sliced

FOR SERVING:

Bread and butter

Cover the pot and cook in the oven 2½ hours; if the meat is not tender at that point, cook until it's tender.

Let the stew cool, then refrigerate 24 hours. You always want to serve stews the next day—it really makes a big difference. The taste and consistency is always deepened.

Make the horseradish bacon-creamed fingerling smashed potatoes: Place the potatoes in a large pot and fill with cold water; add salt. Bring to a boil and cook until fork-tender, 15 minutes. Drain and set aside. (The potatoes can keep in the fridge for up to 3 days.)

In a large pan set over medium-high heat, cook the bacon and render until crisp and there's plenty of fat. Pinch the potatoes with your fingers so they are smashed, bursting them open, so they can get crisp and crunchy in the bacon fat. Add to the pan and cook, about 2 minutes per side, flipping so they are crisp on both sides. Add the horseradish and cream; reduce until it looks like bacon-potato porridge, 1 to 2 minutes, then add some salt, if needed, a bunch of pepper, and a ton of green onions.

Serve the potatoes alongside the stew. Grill some bread and serve with cold butter.

Note: When reheating the stew, do it slowly—there's a lot of fat and collagen that takes time to warm up. Always start over low heat and add a little water to help at the beginning. Adding water will not dilute the stew. You can also stir in some butter, if you're really feeling gully.

Double-Bone Pork Chop with
Maple Jack Daniel's Bacon Sauce

—

SERVES: 4

PREP TIME: 2 DAYS PLUS
30 MINUTES

—

10% brine (page 182)

1 (15-ounce/430 g) double-bone center-cut pork chop

½ pound (225 g) slab bacon, diced

4 cloves garlic, peeled and minced

1 shallot, peeled and diced

2 tablespoons Jack Daniel's whiskey

3 tablespoons maple syrup

1 tablespoon Kozlik's Canadian Mustard (Triple Crunch) or another kind of grainy mustard

¼ cup (60 ml) demi-glace

Juice of 1 lemon

Canola oil

3 tablespoons unsalted butter

1 tablespoon thyme leaves

1 tablespoon rosemary

There's nothing more Canadian than covering a pork chop with a maple bacon sauce. This is a dish that people still ask me about nine years after we opened. I'm talking about you, Junzy! Maybe just one person, but still . . . the salty, fatty, crispy, molasses-y, Jacky-mustardy sauce is what really made this pork chop. The chop itself was a great piece of meat (by no means, don't let me mislead you), but if you put that sauce on a burning diaper filled with baby shit, you would be sucking that sauce off it like a soup dumpling from Chinatown.

Ask your butcher for a center-cut double-bone 15-ounce (430 g) pork chop. This is the Rolls-Royce of pork chops. Also ask to keep a fat cap on—tell him not to trim that fat too much.

—

Brine the pork chop 24 hours (see page 182). Dry the pork chop with paper towels and air-dry 24 hours on a wire rack set on a baking sheet in the refrigerator. (Do not season with salt and pepper.)

In a medium pan set over medium heat, cook the bacon until golden and crisp, 10 minutes. Add 1 clove of the garlic and the shallot; deglaze with the whiskey, maple syrup, and mustard, and finally, add the demi-glace. Cook 10 minutes; you will know it's ready when it bubbles up like caramel. Add the lemon juice, and if it's too thick, add a few tablespoons of water. Keep warm on the stove.

In a cast-iron pan set over medium heat, pour ½ inch (12 mm) of oil; sear the pork chop on both sides until golden brown, 5 minutes per side. Pour out half the oil, return the pan to the stove, and add the butter, the remaining garlic, and the thyme and rosemary. Baste the pork chop with a spoon and cook 3 minutes per side 3 times, flipping 6 times total, basting continuously. When done, place on a rack on top of a baking sheet and pour the butter over it. Let the pork chop rest at least 10 minutes before serving.

Pour all the sauce on a plate, then carve the pork chop, fan it out, and display the beauty.

Buffaloaf

SERVES: 4
PREP TIME: 2 HOURS

2 tablespoons unsalted butter, plus more for the loaf pan

2 tablespoons canola oil

1 onion, finely diced

1 leek, cleaned and finely diced

3 cloves garlic, peeled and minced

2 pounds (910 g) ground bison meat

½ pound (225 g) ground pork back fat

1 cup (240 ml) ketchup

3 eggs

1 cup (100 g) dry bread crumbs

3 tablespoons tomato paste

2 tablespoons chopped sage

2 tablespoons chopped parsley

2 tablespoons (34 g) kosher salt

25 cracks fresh black pepper

Buuufffffaaallllllloooooooaaafffff! What the fuck is Buffaloaf? The idea was water buffalo meat loaf. We came up with this name the same way we did with many dishes at Oddfellows—over beers and lots of smokes. We would always have a name for a dish before the dish itself. Most of the dishes came from jokes, inside jokes, or just complete stupidity. The hardest part of all of this was trying to remember the next day . . . what were we talking about last night at 4 A.M.? Making meat loaf out of water buffalo and calling it buffaloaf? We planned this all out very meticulously. We wanted to serve it on a jail-style square plate: a nice square of buffaloaf, cream corn, mashed potatoes, roasted mushrooms, tomato conserve and gravy, and maybe some carrots. With this came many questions: How can we get jail-style plates? How do we get water buffalo meat? Will people eat buffaloaf? Has this idea gone too far? Are we completely insane? Have we become unhinged? No way! Everyone will love buffaloaf as much as we do! And we will become rich, successful restaurateurs because of this buffaloaf! I'm pretty sure we weren't the first people to think that we could get rich off a meat loaf . . . or were we?

You can only find water buffalo in Africa or Asia, so more likely you're going to use bison. If you can't find that, you can use beef or whatever red meat you want. I think meat loaf done really well is an incredible classic, and everyone should know how to make it.

If you're lucky enough to have a proper butcher, he or she can grind the meat for you (and you can ask to have ground pork back fat added to the mixture). But if you have a meat grinder at home, cube the meat and pork back fat and place in the freezer for thirty minutes before grinding.

In a medium pan set over medium-high heat, melt the butter and oil. Add the onion, leek, and garlic and caramelize them nicely, about 10 minutes. Remove from the heat and pour into a bowl; cool to room temperature, then place in the fridge 30 minutes.

Preheat the oven to 350°F (175°C). Now we make a giant meatball: In a large stainless-steel bowl, place the bison and pork fat and add the cooked onions, leeks, and garlic with all the fats and oils. Add ¾ cup (180 ml) of the ketchup, the eggs, bread crumbs, tomato paste, sage, parsley, salt, and pepper. Mix together and work it like a giant meatball.

Heavily butter a 9¼ by 5¼-inch (23.5 by 13.3 cm) loaf pan, then line it with parchment paper. Fill it to the top with the meat, making sure it's as tight as you can get it. Bang the pan against the counter a few times to get out the air bubbles and to make it compact. Cover the top of the buffaloaf with the remaining ketchup.

Bake in the oven until a thermometer inserted into the meat registers 145°F (63°C), about 45 minutes, then remove from the oven and let cool 20 minutes before you slice a perfect piece of buffaloaf.

Tempeh Clubhouse Sandwich

SERVES: 6

PREP TIME: 1 HOUR AND 30
MINUTES PLUS 1 DAY RESTING

**FOR THE PORTOBELLOS
AND TEMPEH:**

6 portobello mushrooms, stems
and gills removed

1 cup (240 ml) good soy sauce

3 cloves garlic, peeled and minced

1 medium knob ginger, peeled

¼ cup (60 ml) rice wine vinegar

6 dried shiitake mushrooms

3 tablespoons sambal

4 green onions, chopped

½ cup (120 ml) olive oil

1 pound (455 g) tempeh, sliced
into 6 portions

FOR THE RRP BBQ SAUCE:

3 tablespoons canola oil

1 onion, peeled and sliced
lengthwise

4 cloves garlic, peeled and minced

3 roasted red peppers, sliced
lengthwise

1 cup (240 ml) ketchup

½ cup (120 ml) molasses

1 cup (240 ml) apple cider vinegar

¼ cup (50 g) granulated sugar

2 tablespoons smoked paprika

1 tablespoon dry mustard

1 tablespoon ground cumin

1 tablespoon ground coriander

1 tablespoon ground ginger

1 tablespoon dried red chile
flakes

Ingredients continue

I'm indifferent to veganism. I never understood the mock-meat thing. If you were a vegan, wouldn't you just want to eat vegetables? I totally respect someone who has the willpower to never eat a pepperoni pizza or a cheeseburger. A lot of my friends were vegan at one point. So when I opened Oddfellows, my best friend, Liam, asked if I would make a vegan club sandwich. This tempeh club made vegans really happy and made me very upset. It was such a pain to make during service.

Our dishwasher at Oddfellows was Jesse B. Harris, who is an unreal artist and an amazing partner to Michelle and a father to Salvatore Zoo. He was the real MVP and became a pro at making and assembling these sandwiches. We would often find ourselves crushed during service trying to make six club sandwiches. It would shut down the kitchen. Our kitchen was so small, we would have baking sheets on the top of the dishwasher to use to assemble these clubs. I would grill the tempeh, portobello mushroom, and bread. Jesse would assemble the whipped avocado, alfalfa, tomato, lettuce, and onion. For a small three-man team, Mattitude, Jesse, and I crushed those vegans with the best vegan sandwich they ever ate. Vegans can't keep things simple—just make a sandwich with grilled vegetables and smash.

—

Make the portobellos and tempeh: Preheat the oven to 350°F (175°C). Put the portobellos in a deep baking dish and pour in the soy sauce, 2 cups (480 ml) water, the garlic, ginger, rice wine vinegar, shiitakes, sambal, green onions, and oil. Swish it all around, wrap the baking dish in aluminum foil, and cook in the oven 30 minutes. Remove from the oven and let cool to room temperature. Put the portobellos and tempeh in a small container; ladle some of the liquid over them, cover and place in the fridge 24 hours.

Make the RRP BBQ sauce: In a medium saucepan set over medium heat, pour the oil and cook the onion and garlic until caramelized, about 5 minutes. Add the roasted red peppers, ketchup, molasses, apple cider vinegar, sugar, paprika, dry mustard, cumin, coriander, ginger, and chile flakes; bring to a boil. Add 2 cups (480 ml) water and simmer 45 minutes. Transfer to a blender and blend until smooth. (Make sure to fill the blender only halfway so it doesn't explode all over you and your kitchen. If you have a hand blender, you can use that.) Let cool, then pour into a container, cover, and place in the refrigerator 24 hours.

Make the pickled red onion: Place the onion in a mixing bowl; add the salt, sugar, lemon juice, and white vinegar. With your hands, mix and massage the onions, then submerge them (as they start to pickle, they will release water). Let sit 1 hour (you can mix until they start to turn pink). This is a very quick easy pickle. When the onions start turning bright pink, place them in the fridge.

Recipe continues

1 red onion, sliced into medium rounds

Pinch kosher salt

1 tablespoon granulated sugar

Juice of 1 lemon

2 tablespoons white vinegar

FOR THE WHIPPED AVOCADO:

1 avocado

1 cup (250 g) soft tofu

Zest and juice of 2 limes

1 cup (240 ml) olive oil

Kosher salt

FOR ASSEMBLING THE TEMPEH CLUBHOUSE SANDWICH:

Kosher salt and freshly ground black pepper

12 slices whole-wheat bread

Olive oil

Butter bib lettuce leaves

1 heirloom tomato, sliced

Alfalfa sprouts

Olives, for garnish

Pickled hot peppers, for garnish

Make the whipped avocado: Place the avocado and tofu in a food processor. Add the lime zest and juice and blend. Pour in the oil in a single slow stream, processing. Add salt to taste and place in an airtight container in the refrigerator. Put the pit of the avocado in the container to help with oxidation.

Make the sandwich: Preheat the broiler and place a rack in the middle of the oven. Drain the tempeh and portobellos and put them on a baking sheet; season with salt and pepper. Place the baking sheet in the oven and let the tempeh and portobellos get some color, 5 minutes. Be careful not to burn them! Add the RRP BBQ sauce on the tempeh, then return to the oven to scorch the top of the BBQ sauce. Remove from the oven and put the mushrooms on top of the tempeh.

Broil the bread, drizzle with some oil, and sprinkle with salt and pepper.

Spoon a good amount of whipped avocado on two slices of bread, then add lettuce and tomato on the bottom; season with salt and pepper. Place the tempeh with the portobello on top, then add a bunch of pickled red onions. Top with a fluffy layer of alfalfa sprouts and the second slice of bread. Cut the sandwich in half and skewer with an olive and pickled hot pepper. Now make six of these at once without Jesse B. Harris. Good luck.

Coca-Cola Pork Belly and Grilled Short Ribs

—

SERVES: 4

PREP TIME: 1 DAY PLUS
2 HOURS

—

FOR THE BEEF SHORT RIBS:

10% brine (page 182)

2 (6-inch/15 cm) beef short ribs

2 cups (480 ml) red wine

½ cup (120 ml) soy sauce

½ cup (120 ml) maple syrup

1 cup (240 ml) ketchup

½ cup (120 ml) yellow mustard

1 onion, chopped

1 carrot, peeled and chopped

1 stalk celery, chopped

3 cloves garlic, peeled

2 tablespoons ground cumin

2 tablespoons ground cardamom

2 tablespoons ground coriander

2 tablespoons smoked paprika

2 bay leaves

1 bunch parsley

1 bunch thyme

½ cup (120 ml) white vinegar

Ingredients continue

I'm not sure what technique this is, but grilling raw pork belly pretty much until it's burnt, then braising it in a Coca-Cola–soy sauce mixture for a few hours, then grilling it again turns out to be okay. The short rib came after, with just a simple French-style browning and braising in red wine, and then we made a barbecue sauce for it. I'm not sure why I thought Asian pork belly with French beef short rib covered in barbecue sauce would be good, but it sold a lot and people loved this dish.

We served it with a parsnip puree and grilled green onions and a Chinese-style condiment with ginger, green onions, and salt. This dish sums up Oddfellows to me: The restaurant wrote its own rules, and it was one of a kind. And it definitely did not care what people thought. Co-owner Kei Ng taught me a lot, and this pork belly technique was one of them. He's from Malaysia, and this is not a family secret or anything like that—this dish is purely wild style. To this day, my wife wants me to make it, and I still have never made it at home! Writing this story really got me thinking about it, so maybe now I'll cook it. This is very easy if you have a grill; if you don't, just use a cast-iron pan like you would with the short rib.

—

Make the short ribs: Brine the ribs (see page 182) for at least 24 hours.

Preheat the oven to 300°F (150°C). Place the short ribs in a Dutch oven and add 4 cups (960 ml) water, the wine, soy sauce, maple syrup, ketchup, mustard, onion, carrot, celery, garlic, cumin, cardamom, coriander, paprika, bay leaves, parsley, and thyme. Bring to a boil and cover; roast in the oven 2½ to 3 hours. (You can do this at the same time the pork belly is being braised.)

Remove the short ribs from the Dutch oven when the meat is tender but before it's falling off the bone. Place the braising sauce in a blender and blend, adding the vinegar. Pass the sauce through a fine sieve. Put the short ribs in a container, cover with sauce, and refrigerate for 24 hours.

In a medium pan set over medium heat, warm the short ribs in the sauce. Remove the short ribs from the sauce and grill lightly and slowly while basting with the sauce. We are just looking to add a nice glaze, so about 2 minutes per side and keep it moving.

Make the pork belly: In a blender, place the garlic, ginger, cilantro, and green onions and blend to a pulp. Transfer to a large bowl and pour in the Coca-Cola, soy sauce, and 2 cups (480 ml) water. Place the pork belly in the marinade and refrigerate 24 hours.

Recipe continues

FOR THE PORK BELLY:

4 cloves garlic, peeled

1 knob ginger, peeled

½ bunch cilantro

4 green onions

2 (16-ounce/475 ml) cans Coca-Cola

1 cup (240 ml) soy sauce

2 pounds (910 g) skin-on pork belly

8 dried shiitake mushrooms

FOR THE PARSNIP PUREE:

4 parsnips, peeled and cut into 1-inch (2.5 cm) cubes

Heavy cream

¼ cup (60 ml) maple syrup

¼ cup (½ stick/55 g) unsalted butter

FOR THE GRILLED ONIONS:

12 green onions

Juice of ½ lemon

1 tablespoon olive oil

Remove the pork belly from the marinade and get your grill really hot. Blacken the outside of the pork belly all the way around, about 5 minutes a side. The sugar from the marinade should make this pretty easy. Return the pork belly to the marinade, which will now turn into the braising liquid. Add the mushrooms.

Preheat the oven to 350°F (175°C). Place the pork belly and liquid on a baking dish with aluminum foil. Cover with more foil and braise in the oven 2½ hours.

The pork belly is done when you can stick a wooden skewer through it with just a little resistance. Remove the aluminum foil cover and let cool to room temperature. Remove the pork belly and place in another bowl; strain the braising liquid over it and discard the solids. Wrap the bowl with plastic wrap and place in the fridge 24 hours.

The next day, remove the pork belly from the braising liquid and portion into 4-ounce (115 g) pieces. Warm the braising liquid and use it as a glaze when you grill the meat. Gently grill the pork belly until it's crisp and fatty, about 5 minutes per side, and brush the glaze over it with a pastry brush.

Make the parsnip puree: Place the parsnips in a pot and add just enough cream to cover; bring to a boil, then simmer until the parsnips are fork-tender, 15 minutes. Transfer the parsnips to a blender; add the maple syrup and butter and blend until smooth. If desired, strain through a chinois.

Make the grilled onions: Grill green onions until wilted and mix with the lemon juice and olive oil.

To plate: Slice the pork belly and the short ribs; serve with a bowl of parsnip puree and green onions.

Grilled Quail with Smoked Quail Eggs

SERVES: 5

PREP TIME: 2 HOURS PLUS
AN OVERNIGHT BRINE

**FOR THE GRILLED QUAIL
AND HERB MARINADE:**

5 quails

10% brine (page 182)

½ bunch parsley, finely chopped

½ bunch tarragon, finely
chopped

½ bunch basil, finely chopped

½ bunch mint, finely chopped

½ bunch cilantro, finely chopped

½ bunch chervil, finely chopped

2 tablespoons peeled and
minced garlic

1 shallot, peeled and minced

Olive oil

Zest and juice of 1 orange

Zest and juice of 1 lemon

3 mandarin oranges, halved

FOR THE TARTAR SAUCE:

2 quail eggs

1 stalk celery, diced

1 shallot, peeled and diced

8 cornichons, diced

2 green onions, thinly sliced

1 cup (240 ml) mayonnaise

½ tablespoon chopped tarragon

½ tablespoon chopped chervil

½ tablespoon chopped parsley

Zest and juice of 1 orange

Zest and juice of 1 lemon

Kosher salt and freshly ground
black pepper

Quail is sick. Oddfellows was sick. At Oddies we didn't have a lot of space so quail made more sense to serve than chicken. Having quail on the menu was all about time and efficiency. It was great that we could throw a few on the grill and serve them up quickly. Do what we did: grill some quails, make some tartar sauce, and have at it!

—

Make the quail: Cut each quail in half with kitchen scissors and brine (see page 182) for 24 hours.

Make the herb marinade: In a bowl, place the parsley, tarragon, basil, mint, cilantro, chervil, garlic, and shallot; cover with oil, and add the zest and juice of the orange and lemon.

Cover the quails with the marinade, then lay them flat on a baking sheet and let sit in the fridge 1 hour. Remove from the fridge 30 minutes before grilling.

On a hot grill, grill the quails skin side down first. You want to let them cook quickly, so don't move them right away—you want them to get some color before turning. Cook them most of the way on the skin side, then flip the birds over to the meat side and cook until medium, about 3 minutes a side. I like a lot of char on this dish. As the quails are grilling, grill the oranges cut side down until charred and dripping with hot, acidic, sweet juice.

Allow the quails to rest a few minutes. Dip in the juice from the oranges and a liberal amount of the smoky, tangy tartar sauce (recipe follows).

Make the tartar sauce: If you have a smoker, get it smoking with your favorite wood. Pour 4 cups (960 ml) water into a heatproof bowl. Smoke the water 1 hour, then strain the water through cheesecloth and place in the fridge. If you don't have a smoker, don't worry—just skip this step.

Bring a small pot of water to boil; once it's boiling, add the eggs and cook 4 minutes, then place directly into an ice bath. Let cool. Carefully peel the eggs, then place them in the smoked water 24 hours in the fridge. As is, these smoked quail eggs are the perfect snack. If you don't have a smoker, don't worry—regular eggs will be fine.

Place the celery, shallot, cornichons, and green onions in a bowl. Remove the quail eggs from the water, drip dry, and cut in half and then into quarters. Place the diced eggs in the bowl and add mayonnaise to combine all the ingredients; you want it to look lumpy. Add the herbs to the mixture, along with the zest and juice of the orange and lemon. Season with a pinch of salt and a few cracks of pepper.

Grilled Fermented Black Bean Flat-Iron Steak with Nước Chấm

SERVES: 4

PREP TIME: 30 MINUTES, PLUS
24 HOURS MARINATING

**FOR THE MARINADE
AND STEAK:**

1 cup (185 g) fermented black beans (found in a Chinatown store or on the dark web, hopefully)

8 cloves garlic, peeled

1 knob ginger, peeled

1 bunch cilantro

Canola oil

1 cup (240 ml) soy sauce

½ cup (120 ml) ketchup

½ cup (120 ml) hoisin sauce

4 (6-ounce) flat-iron steaks

FOR THE NƯỚC CHẤM:

10 Thai bird's eye chile peppers

1 knob ginger, peeled

4 cloves garlic, peeled

3 tablespoons palm sugar

Roots of 1 bunch cilantro

½ cup (120 ml) fish sauce

1 teaspoon brandy

2 tablespoons rice wine vinegar

Zest and juice of 3 limes

Stems of 1 bunch cilantro

Olive oil (optional)

When Kei Ng was the chef at the restaurant that bore his name, he made a classic steak dish that was fermented in black bean puree and served with a fish sauce dipping sauce. We changed a few things when we brought the dish to Oddfellows, but it was pretty much the same. The fermented black bean puree marinade was pretty intense and made this steak an umami grenade, and the super-punchy fish sauce dip put it over the top. It was on the menu for only the first few months because it really didn't fit everything on our "Canadian" menu. We had this bright acidic Malaysian-style grilled steak floating on a menu of a lot of heavy foods. It's tough taking some things off the menu, but this just interrupted the flow. A lot of people didn't like grilled steak and spicy fish sauce ten years ago, I guess. Now that dish would be on fire. One more reason Oddfellows was ahead of its time. The sauce was a Mattitude creation—the base was Thai bird's eye chiles, the cilantro roots, fish sauce, and palm sugar. We are not going to be seasoning with salt because the marinade is quite salty and so is the fish sauce.

Make the marinade: Put the beans in a blender. Bring 3 cups (720 ml) water to a boil, then pour over the beans; let sit 30 minutes. Add the garlic, ginger, cilantro, 1 cup (240 ml) oil, the soy sauce, ketchup, and hoisin sauce. Blend until smooth.

Place the steaks in a baking dish and pour the marinade over them. Cover the dish in plastic wrap and refrigerate 24 hours.

Make the nước chấm: With a large mortar and pestle, smash the chiles, ginger, garlic, sugar, and cilantro roots until the mixture has the consistency of pulp. Place in a bowl and add the fish sauce, brandy, vinegar, 2 cups (480 ml) water, and the lime zest and juice.

Slice the cilantro stems as you would chives and add to the sauce and stir. If it needs a little fat, you can add some oil as well. Keep the sauce in a container, and before serving, shake. The sauce keeps in the refrigerator for 3 to 4 days.

Make the steaks: Wipe off the steaks with your hands. If desired, rub in some canola oil. Place them on a plate.

Get your grill nice and hot and place your steaks lined up at the two o'clock position; after 3 minutes, turn the steaks to the eleven o'clock position (this will give you nice grill marks). Then flip to the other side and repeat. Six minutes per side should do the trick. Let the steaks rest, about 10 minutes, then slice against the grain and place on a plate.

Serve the steaks with the nước chấm.

"This Wheel's on Fire"

Parts & Labour

*Opening night at Parts & Labour when I was twenty-seven; walking by the customers,
stressed out and giving cut eye. Lisa Canamoto in the foreground, poorly taking a drink order.*

The magic that many never understood or loved to hate

ODDFELLOWS ON ACID WAS
OUR BUSINESS PLAN

Parts & Labour came from Kei Ng and Brian Richer of Oddfellows teaming up with Jesse Girard and Richard Lambert from a nightclub called The Social to open up a restaurant in the neighborhood of Parkdale. Trust me: Opening a restaurant in Parkdale in 2010 was a crazy idea and still is to this day. I had been living in the neighborhood since 2004, and it had only two chef-driven restaurants, the Cowbell and Local Kitchen and Wine Bar. Everything else was a dive bar or diner. Brian and Kei were to design and execute the build-out, and Jesse and Richard were to be the operators, running the day-to-day business.

Oddfellows was still going strong two kilometers east of where Parts & Labour would open. The original idea for Parts & Labour was to scale up and try to do Oddfellows on acid. With twenty-six seats and a twenty-six-year-old cokehead chef, Oddfellows was doomed from the beginning. So naturally, we thought opening a bigger one would be a great idea.

At Parts & Labour, we wanted to have live punk music in the basement and contemporary French food with unpretentious service upstairs. We had a rooftop garden that we called Parks & Rec. Katie Mathieu was our permaculture designer and Victoria Taylor was our landscape architect. They created an amazing 1,800-square-foot organic garden, where we grew carrots, radishes, and many other things. It ended when our neighbor ratted us out to the building inspector and our garden was deemed an illegal structure. It was nice to get three summers out of it.

While working on this book, my friend and three-year-suffering cook at the restaurant Alex Goodall reminded me of the time I came back from cooking at a dinner with the Group of Seven Chefs at the James Beard house in New York. It was a big deal for me. We were the first Canadians ever to cook there. I came back with a newfound pride for my work as a chef. I was drinking my own Kool-Aid; the ego was really setting in at this moment.

The Group of Seven Chefs had a celebratory dinner at Per Se in New York City. We were all talking about how the restaurant has SENSE OF URGENCY signs hanging in their kitchen under each clock as a mantra for the standards they want to maintain. I loved it, so I came up with my own for Parts & Labour. When I returned, I stuck a large piece of masking tape on the pass (where we would keep our food orders) and wrote a phrase on it. Full of pride, I showed my brigade the new sign:

N-O C-O-M-P-R-I-S-E

No Comprise. My misspelled version of No Compromises. Even though it was misspelled it hung in the kitchen for weeks. It was a perfect metaphor of what P&L was. A restaurant trying to be what it wasn't. We just weren't those kinds of chefs.

I fucked up by thinking we could serve that kind of food in that space. It didn't work. Within a year and a half we had to change our menu format and way of service. Our food and staff costs were way too high for the kind of business that we were doing. In what world do you think we could be serving horse tenderloin and elk tartare to a large number of customers blasting music, trying to get them drunk on whiskey? Our original menu format was appetizer, main course, and dessert. We could not execute at the level we wanted with the staff we had. Because we had large communal tables, every single table turned into Chuck E. Cheese's; every table was a birthday party of at least ten people. Cooking main courses for ten to twelve tables at one time meant being backed up so badly that some tables would have to wait almost two hours for a main course. We had to change. It was too intense for that style of cooking.

Parts & Labour was crazy during this time. Everyone on staff was partying till five in the morning, every night. Parts & Labour became more than Oddfellows on acid. It became a monster that we couldn't control. Finally, everything caught up with me. I was exhausted from trying to make the restaurant the best I could and from partying harder than I ever had before, if you can believe that. And then it all came to a screeching halt after a three-day bender of no sleep, drinkin', and druggin'. I had a heart attack. I was crushed. I thought the ride was over.

The doctor told me to take three months off. That did not happen. After being in the hospital for five days, I was back at work within ten. As a lot of people in the industry know, it is very difficult for chefs to take any time off, let alone three months. We had a lot of steam, and everything was going well. P&L Catering was about to launch, and the restaurant was as busy as ever. I did end up not drinking or doing drugs for three months. I had a lot of pressure to get back to work. Then one night I had a drink, and all of a sudden, I was back in the grips of partying for about two years. I manipulated, stole, lied. I was running the restaurant and doing what I had to do to survive: lying, hiding, and going places I'd never been before. My friends, my girlfriend, and everyone were worried about me. I didn't care that I'd had a heart attack but everyone else did. I felt that I was invincible. My old drug dealers wouldn't sell me drugs because they didn't want me to die on their bag. I started going to different bars, and I started getting different drug dealers. I didn't want the party to be over, but it was for everyone else.

Juxtaposition of flowers and indulgences

Richard, Kei, Brian, and Jesse were growing up and trying to make Parts &
Labour a really good restaurant. And I kept on being the kid. I pushed their
patience to its end and they were tired of Matty fucking everything up.

There was an intervention. It was Richard, Hambone, Wade, and Benny,
and they just said, "You're done." And I said, "Okay, I'm done." We talked
for hours. The next day I went to my first meeting. I haven't had a drop in
almost five years.

I was still working every day and going to a meeting every day. They
were so understanding. If a meeting was at 8 P.M. during service, they
would let me leave and come back. They always told me, Whatever you
need to do to not die. It was life or death, it was friendship over business,
as it always had been.

During this time I started doing stuff for Vice. At first, I taped a small
series of shows for Munchies called *Hangover Cures*. After I got sober, I
called Patrick McGuire to tell him I couldn't tape a show where I drank
anymore. Vice said, No problem, and we developed a how-to video for
making a burger. I couldn't believe it. I got paid $500 for taping that thing,
which is the most money I ever made in one day up to that point. It now
has over six million views on YouTube. That led to even more how-to
videos on everything from pancakes to mac and cheese with Cheetos on
top to the online show *Keep It Canada*, which combined touring Canada
and hanging out with local chefs and purveyors. I couldn't believe it—I was
getting paid to travel across Canada and hang out with my chef buddies.

It was obvious, within a year and a half of shooting Hangover Cures,
How-tos, and *Keep It Canada*, Vice started pulling me away from the daily
operations of the restaurant. And that was before Viceland offered me *Dead
Set on Life*, where I traveled the world six months out of the year. Shooting
that show was an incredible opportunity. All of a sudden, I became a celebrity chef guy. I was booking appearances and dinners. And P&L started
to feel like a job I wasn't doing properly. Brent Pierssens, who has been at
P&L since day one, became chef de cuisine and started running the day-
to-day, and I became the face for a year and a half. As *Dead Set on Life* and
eventually *It's Suppertime!* started to take up an even larger part of my time,
I felt like it was disrespectful to take Kei, Brian, Jesse, and Richard's money
when I wasn't there. It crushed me but we all knew it was time for me to
move on from Parts & Labour. It was not the same restaurant we opened
nine years before and I was not the same person. I owe them literally everything. I love you guys.

Elk Loin, Carrots, and Celeriac with Pickled Blueberries

—

SERVES: 2

PREP TIME: 1 DAY, PLUS 30
MINUTES

—

**FOR THE PICKLED
BLUEBERRIES:**

½ cup (100 g) granulated sugar

1 cup (240 ml) white vinegar

1 cup (240 ml) dry white wine

3 pints (435 g) blueberries
(preferably wild-picked)

FOR THE CELERIAC PUREE:

3 celery roots, peeled and
quartered

½ cup (120 ml) heavy cream

¼ cup (60 ml) maple syrup

½ cup (1 stick/115 g) cold
unsalted butter, cubed

Kosher salt

FOR THE CARROTS:

2 bunches nice baby carrots
with tops

2 tablespoons canola oil

1 shallot, peeled and diced

¼ cup (60 ml) red wine vinegar

¼ cup (60 ml) maple syrup

2 tablespoons unsalted butter

Kosher salt and freshly ground
black pepper

Ingredients continue

For some reason, I thought pickled blueberries were cool. If you ate at Parts & Labour during our first few months, it was a little rough. We were serving food that was maybe not the perfect fit for the room, but I loved these perfect little blueberries on anything, especially roasted elk loin.

This is one of those very straightforward dishes that we tried to make complex with the plating. We served it on a wooden cutting board because . . . why not? It's funny to look back at trends from nine years ago. Back then, everyone was serving everything on wooden boards. We just drank the Kool-Aid and put pickled blueberries with elk on a wooden board. I was immature; I could have avoided being some trend-jumping punk chef and just served it on a plate like an adult.

—

Make the pickled blueberries: In a large pot, combine the sugar, vinegar, wine, and 2 cups (480 ml) water; bring to a boil. Let cool to room temperature and pour over the blueberries in a bowl; refrigerate 24 hours.

Make the celeriac puree: Bring a medium pot of salted water to a boil; add the celery root and cook until fork-tender, about 15 minutes.

Transfer the celery root to a blender and pulse, then add some of the cream and maple syrup (to taste), then add the cubed butter. You will need to eye this because you want it to be a nice, smooth puree—stiff but still very smooth. Pass the puree through a fine chinois, then place in a saucepan over low heat until needed for plating. Season with salt to taste.

Make the carrots: Cut off the tops of the carrots, leaving ½ inch (12 mm) of greens. With the tip of a paring knife, scrape around the edges of the carrots to remove the dirt from around the greens, then scrub the carrots under cold water. You don't have to peel the carrots.

Heat the oil in a medium pan over medium-high heat and drop in your carrots. Scorch them, then add the shallot. Add the vinegar to deglaze and reduce by half, then add the maple syrup and butter and season with salt and pepper to taste; swirl the pan and this will become agrodolce, so to speak—the sweet and the sour and the butter will make almost a caramel sauce that will surround the carrots and make them very desirable. We are cooking them for about 15 minutes total and leaving them in the pan to keep them warm.

Recipe continues

2 (4-ounce/115 g) elk loins

Kosher salt and freshly ground black pepper

¼ cup (60 ml) canola oil

FOR THE DEMI-GLACE:

1 cup (240 ml) demi-glace

3 tablespoons unsalted butter

Juice of 1 lemon

Kosher salt and freshly ground black pepper

Sprigs of parsley, for garnish

Cook the elk: Preheat the oven to 350°F (175°C). There is no fat on elk loin, so it's difficult to cook it evenly and make sure that it's not dry. When dealing with a lean meat, letting it temper is key—sear it quickly and place it in the oven for just a few minutes to heat through. (Also, letting lean meat rest is very important.) Set a cast-iron pan over medium-high heat (the pan should not be smoking, just hot). Season the elk with salt and pepper, then pour the oil in the pan and place in the elk. Sear until golden brown, 1 minute on each side.

Place the elk on a rack set on a baking sheet and cook in the oven 3 minutes. Remove and tent with aluminum foil; let rest 10 minutes.

Make the demi-glace: In a small pot over medium heat, heat the demi-glace, butter, lemon juice, salt, and pepper. Whisk to combine. Turn off the heat and keep ready to plate.

Spoon some celeriac puree and carrots on a plate. Slice the elk and fan. Cover with the demi-glace and decorate with the parsley.

Grilled Quail with Vegetable Succotash

—

SERVES: 2

PREP TIME: 1 DAY PLUS
30 MINUTES

—

FOR THE QUAIL:

2 quails

½ cup (120 g) kosher salt

2 tablespoons sugar

4 sprigs thyme

2 bay leaves

2 cloves garlic, peeled

Zest of 1 orange

FOR THE HONEY BUTTER:

¼ cup (60 ml) good honey

¼ cup (½ stick/55 g) cold
unsalted butter, cubed

2 sprigs thyme, leaves picked

½ clove garlic

Zest of ½ lemon

FOR THE VEGETABLE
SUCCOTASH:

4 quarts (3.8 L) chicken stock

4 pearl onions, peeled and
chopped

3 pattypan squash, chopped

2 baby zucchini, chopped

1 long garlic scape, chopped

2 baby leeks, cleaned

½ cup (60 g) diced butternut
squash

3 cremini mushrooms, chopped

Ingredients continue

This dish was served during the summer months at Parts & Labour. It was a beautiful dish. We had a rooftop garden at this point and were getting some amazing vegetables: radishes, carrots, lettuce, peppers, cucumbers. But don't worry: You don't need a rooftop garden. This recipe is very adaptable. In the winter you could use squash, beets, rutabaga, and turnips—it's pretty much just a bunch of vegetables chopped and cooked down quickly with chicken jus and mustard seeds. It makes a great bed for a charred honey-basted bird to lay to rest. People always wanted a burger at Parts & Labour, but we had such great dishes like this one. I hope this recipe connects you with vegetables.

—

Make the quail: When you get the whole quails, hopefully they have their feet and heads attached. You can cut off the heads and discard, or you could cut them in half and simmer them in the chicken jus for the vegetable succotash. Cut the spine from the birds with good kitchen scissors so you can grill them flat.

In a food processor, make the salt cure: Combine the salt, sugar, thyme, bay leaves, garlic, and orange zest; process until fully incorporated.

In a baking dish, make a little salt-cure bed about ¼ inch (6 mm) thick for your quails to lie on, meat side down. Push the quails onto the cure and sprinkle a little of the cure on the skin side as well. Massage the cure into the skin, then cover with plastic wrap and refrigerate 3 hours. Remove the quails and brush off the cure. Tie the feet of the quails and hang them upside down in the refrigerator 24 hours with a baking sheet or plate underneath to catch any blood or drips.

Make the honey butter: In a medium pot, place the honey, butter, thyme leaves, garlic, and lemon zest and bring to a boil; turn the heat down to low until needed. It should be golden brown and frothy. It's very easy to burn, so keep an eye on this.

Make the vegetable succotash: In a large pot, bring the chicken stock to a boil; reduce to 1 cup (240 ml), about 30 minutes.

In another large pot, place the onions, pattypan squash, zucchini, scape, leeks, butternut squash, mushrooms, and sunchokes. Add the mustard seeds and the reduced chicken stock; bring to a boil. Don't cook for more than 5 minutes—you want the vegetables to still have a crunch. Once it turns to

Recipe continues

3 sunchokes, chopped

1 tablespoon mustard seeds

2 tablespoons Dijon mustard

2 tablespoons unsalted butter

Zest and juice of 1 lemon

Freshly ground black pepper

1 bunch chervil, chopped

1 bunch parsley, chopped

1 bunch tarragon, chopped

1 bunch chives, chopped

FOR SERVING:

1 mandarin orange, lemon,
or lime (optional)

sauce consistency, add the mustard and butter; remove from the heat and stir.

Add the lemon zest and juice, pepper, and a handful of chervil, parsley, tarragon, and chives.

Grill the quail: Heat a grill to high. Remove the quails from the refrigerator and grill flat, skin side down; leave the feet near the edge of the grill so they don't burn, 2 to 3 minutes. Once you get a little color on the skin, flip the quails and start basting with the honey butter. Flip and baste, cooking until the quails are sticky and charred, 6 to 8 minutes total.

Spoon some of the vegetable succotash on a plate, then place 1 quail on top. Squeeze some citrus on top if desired.

The Infamous Fried Pig Face

SERVES: 4
PREP TIME: 5 DAYS

FOR THE HEADCHEESE:

1 pig head

10% brine (page 182)

3 onions, peeled

4 carrots, peeled

4 stalks celery

1 leek, cleaned

1 bunch thyme

1 bunch parsley, chopped

1 bunch tarragon, chopped

4 bay leaves

2 tablespoons coriander seeds

2 tablespoons white pepper-corns

Gelatin sheets, if needed

FOR THE BREADING STATION:

2 cups (250 g) all-purpose flour

4 eggs, whisked

3 cups (240 g) panko bread crumbs

3 cups (720 ml) canola oil

FOR THE MUSTARD-SEED DEMI-GLACE:

3 tablespoons mustard seeds

1 cup (240 ml) demi-glace

Zest and juice of ½ lemon

¼ cup (½ stick/55 g) cold unsalted butter, cubed

Kosher salt and freshly ground black pepper (optional)

Mustard Pickles (page 71), for serving

There's more meat on a pig's head than you would think—you can get about five to seven pounds of meat, fat, and skin from one. It has the most delicious melt-in-your-mouth texture. The jowl, the cheek, the fat, and the skin combine together for something special. This meat can be used in soups, terrines, stews, scrapple, sausage, testina, and so many other amazing dishes.

When we opened Parts & Labour, I decided to serve fried pig face. It was on my first menu draft, it made its way to opening day, and we sold it for two years. This was the only dish that never changed at Parts & Labour. If you want to sell headcheese or *fromage de tête* in your restaurant, it is very difficult. Now, we called it fried pig face, and for some reason everyone wanted it, everyone talked about it, and we sold a lot of it. Little golden nuggets of fried pig face, served with my grandfather's mustard pickles and a mustard-seed demi-glace that just made the dish a home run. If you ever sold headcheese in your restaurant, you also know that it's very good for food cost (not that I knew anything about food cost really at that moment).

I also remember almost every review questioned why we called it pig face. To be honest, I just thought it sounded cool and was a little more original than headcheese. Try to find a butcher who can sell you a pig's head, or even just buy headcheese and you can do everything else. Making headcheese takes five days, so strap yourself in because I'm going to show you how to make this Parts & Labour classic dish. But not really classic because I don't think anything I've ever done is classic. Pretty much everything I've ever cooked has just been pretty much okay.

—

When you buy the pig's head, ask your butcher to shave any extra hairs, and if you get a little scruff, take a disposable razor and shave that piggy for its last time. If the head is not already split, place it on a heavy cutting board facing away from you and, with a heavy weighted cleaver, cut into the top like you're splitting wood. After 4 to 6 whacks, the head should be split. Be mindful of splinters of bone.

Brine the pig's head halves (see page 182); put a plate on top to make sure the head stays in the brine and refrigerate 3 days.

Place the head in another large pot and cover with cold water. Bring to a boil, then pour off the water and scum. Rinse the head quickly with cold water again, then return to the same pot, cover in cold water, and bring to a boil; skim any remaining scum and turn the heat to low and simmer.

Add the onions, carrots, celery, and leek to the pot. Add half the thyme, parsley, and tarragon, the bay leaves, coriander, and peppercorns. Simmer 2½ to 3 hours, until you can puncture all the way through the jowl with a wooden skewer with little resistance. You don't want the meat to fall off

Recipe continues

the bone, and you don't want it cooked too much: You want the jowls to be soft yet firm, the ears just crunchy. This takes time and a very steady simmer.

Remove the head and place in a large container. Carefully remove all the vegetables; place the onions, carrots, and leek on a baking sheet and discard the celery. Through a fine strainer, pour just enough of the cooking liquid to cover the head; cover and refrigerate 24 hours. Pour the remaining liquid into another pot and reduce by half over medium heat. Strain again and let cool, then refrigerate 24 hours (that liquid will become the jelly that holds the headcheese together). If your reduced pig head liquid isn't a thick and tight jelly after 24 hours in the fridge, bring to a boil and add some gelatin sheets—I would add 4 sheets per 1 cup (240 ml) liquid.

Remove the head from the liquid-turned-jelly. Wipe the jelly off the meat with your hands and place the head on a baking sheet skin side down. Using your hands, pull all the meat from the bone, making sure to keep the meat in big pieces. Cut off the ears and julienne; cube the meat, fat, and skin into thumb-size pieces and add to a large baking dish. Dice the carrots, onions, and leek. Add just enough diced vegetables to the baking dish. You want about 4 cups (195 g) chopped pig and 1½ cups (190 g) diced vegetables. Add the remaining parsley and tarragon.

Bring the pot of reduced braising liquid to a boil, then let cool to room temperature. Add just enough liquid to cover the meat. (The meat should almost be floating.) Stir the mixture and wrap the dish with plastic wrap; refrigerate 24 hours to set.

Invert the baking dish onto a baking sheet. With a blow torch, run the flame over the bottom of the dish to release the mixture. Cut into 1-inch (2.5 cm) cubes. Place on a tray and put in the freezer 15 minutes.

Pour the oil into a large pot over medium heat. While the oil is heating, set up a breading station: Place the flour and some salt in a bowl, the eggs in another bowl, and the panko bread crumbs in another bowl. Remove the cubes from the freezer and bread them: First dust in the flour, then dip in the eggs, then coat in the panko, and place on a rack over a baking sheet.

Once the oil has reached a temperature of 320°F (160°C), use a spider to carefully lower a handful of breaded cubes into the hot oil. Cook until golden brown on the outside and molten on the inside, about 5 minutes.

Make the mustard-seed demi-glace: In a small pot over medium heat, place the mustard seeds and demi-glace; melt. Remove from the heat. Add the lemon zest and juice, butter, and salt and pepper, if needed; stir until emulsified.

Open a jar of mustard pickles and strain all the liquid and reserve. Place the pickled veggies in a food processor and blitz once on pulse—you don't want a puree. Transfer to a bowl and add just enough mustard pickle liquid back to the relish.

Spoon some mustard pickle relish and some mustard-seed demi-glace onto a plate and place the crispy hot fried pig face on top.

Roasted Piglet with Sauce Gribiche

SERVES: 6

PREP TIME: 3½ HOURS PLUS
AN OVERNIGHT BRINE

1 leg of a piglet

10% brine (page 182)

4 hard-boiled eggs, separated and diced

2 shallots, peeled and diced

8 cornichons, diced

1 stalk celery, diced

¼ cup (35 g) capers, minced

3 tablespoons Dijon mustard

½ cup (120 ml) champagne vinegar

2 cups (480 ml) canola oil

1 small handful tarragon, chopped

1 small handful Thai basil, chopped

1 small handful Italian basil, chopped

1 small handful cilantro, chopped

1 handful chopped flat-leaf parsley

1 small handful mint, chopped

1 small handful green onions, chopped

Zest and juice of 2 mandarin oranges

Zest and juice of 1 lemon

Freshly ground black pepper

Roasted pork is one of the best things in the world: the cracklings, the fat, the meat. Please find a trusted butcher—he or she has put the time in and gained farmers' trust so that we can enjoy beautifully raised animals. Once you've had a few amazing roasted pork loins, pork ribs, or pork bellies, it's time to talk to your butcher and get some piglet. We would get piglets from Société-Orignal, which was an amazing supplier from Quebec that would sell only the best products. These beautiful pigs would come whole to our restaurant, and we would butcher them into sausage, chops, and roasts, and one lucky table could order the whole roasted head. But my favorite part is roasting a whole front leg and serving it on a large plate lined with a chunky sauce gribiche. I don't like when it is emulsified. I find it's pretty much tartare sauce, which is not great for this dish at all. Maybe if we're making fish and chips. Roasting a piglet's leg is easy and very rewarding. The skin gets so crispy—like glass—the fat is so sweet, and the meat is beyond juicy; it's fucking mental. The trick is to dry out the leg for two days in the fridge, uncovered. This will ensure you get a super-crispy roasted pork leg.

—

Brine the piglet leg (see page 182) for 24 hours.

Place the pig leg on a wire rack on top of a baking sheet lined with paper towels and air-dry for 24 hours. Change the paper towels if any blood drips down. This will dry out the skin, which will make it amazingly crispy.

Preheat the oven to 325°F (165°C). Remove the paper towels from the baking sheet and place the pig leg (with the wire rack and baking sheet) in the oven. Roast 2½ to 3 hours. You'll know it's cooked when you can poke a sharp wooden skewer into the fattest part of the leg and the skewer goes all the way through, like butter. Nothing should stop it; all the connective tissue will be broken down. If you want more color, turn up the heat at the end to 400°F (205°C) until the desired color, about 10 minutes. Blast it, and the skin will get even crispier. Keep an eye on it.

While the pig leg is roasting, make the sauce gribiche: Place the diced egg whites, shallots, cornichons, celery, and capers in a bowl. Place the egg yolks in another large bowl. Add the mustard and vinegar to the egg yolks and whisk until smooth. Then drizzle in the oil and whisk the mixture like your life depends on it. After you've emulsified about 1 cup (240 ml) oil, just pour in the remaining oil and make the sauce split but keep whisking. You now have this really weird separated sauce; add the egg white mixture, the

Recipe continues

tarragon, Thai basil, Italian basil, cilantro, parsley, mint, and green onions to the mixture. Whisk until smooth. Add the zest and juice of the oranges and lemon. Finish with a bunch of salt and pepper.

Remove pig leg from oven and let rest for 20 minutes. If you want to serve this family style, place the roasted leg of piglet on a wooden cutting board with the bowl of sauce gribiche. With the fruity, salty, herby, acidic gribiche, it's a match made in pig heaven. Slice at the table to impress your family and friends.

Pork Ribs with Pig Skin XO Sauce

SERVES: 4

PREP TIME: 3 HOURS,
PLUS 24 HOURS

FOR THE XO SAUCE:

1 cup (200 g) dried shrimp

1 cup (200 g) dried scallops

2 pounds (910 g) fresh pig skin with fat attached, sliced into 3-inch (7.5 cm) strips

¾ cup (100 g) peeled and minced garlic

¾ cup (75 g) minced fresh ginger

¾ cup (25 g) diced lemongrass

¾ cup (65 g) cleaned and diced leeks

1 cup (200 g) diced fermented Chinese sausage

2 cups (480 ml) rendered pork fat

6 tablespoons (90 ml) cognac

½ cup (120 ml) malt vinegar

¼ cup (60 ml) fermented chili paste

1 cup (240 ml) canola oil

2 quarts (2 L) pork stock

½ cup (30 g) thinly sliced scallions (white parts only)

Fish sauce

Canola oil

Ingredients continue

Everyone loves ribs! When I was dreaming up this dish, I wondered, what if you ground boiled pig skin and combined it with XO sauce? Boiled skin is very similar to dried seafood once it has been reconstituted. When we first made this at Parts & Labour, my sous chef Geoff was given the task of working on this, and he killed it. The first time we made it, we nailed it. And that doesn't happen often, let me tell you. It was a huge success in our minds. Now, did the dish sell? Hell, no! Why would anyone buy pig skin XO sauce pork ribs? Even though I was known for selling odd meats, this dish just didn't work, so it didn't last long on the menu. But for some reason, I really loved it. We served it with lightly cured cucumbers and some crème fraîche with a little dusting of homemade chili powder. This XO sauce is great for chicken, fish, roasted squash or pumpkin, dumplings, soup, or even just on some steamed rice.

—

Make the XO sauce: Place the shrimp and scallops in a container and cover with warm tap water; refrigerate 24 hours.

In a large pot, place the pig skin and cold water to cover; bring to a boil, then simmer until tender, 2 hours. Let the skin rest on a baking sheet until it comes to room temperature. Use a large metal spoon to scrape all the fat off the skin (you do not have to be meticulous). Separate the fat and reserve. Slice the skin and cut into a small dice; place in a bowl and reserve.

In a blender, place the garlic, ginger, lemongrass, leeks, and sausage; blend. Transfer the blended mixture to a medium pot; add the rendered pork fat and the scraped pig fat. Cook over medium-low heat until lightly browned, about 10 minutes.

Drain the shrimp and scallops and pulse in a food processor 3 or 4 times. Do not puree. Add to the cooked vegetables and sausage.

Deglaze the pot with the cognac and vinegar; add the chili paste and the oil. Add 1 quart (960 ml) pork stock and reduce by half; cook until the sauce is thick and rich, about 10 minutes. In a bowl, combine the mixture with the pig skin; mix well. While this sauce sits overnight, the skin just absorbs all the flavor. Add the scallions; add fish sauce and oil to taste.

Cover and refrigerate overnight. It will fully set like a brick of butter because of the pork fat. When you want to use some, just spoon a bit out and warm it in a pan until it melts.

Recipe continues

FOR THE PORK RIBS:

1 full rack pork ribs

1 cup (240 ml) hot Chinese mustard

½ cup (50 g) Chinese five-spice powder

FOR THE CUCUMBER SALAD:

1 English cucumber, skin on and chopped

Juice of 2 limes

3 tablespoons rice wine vinegar

Kosher salt

1 tablespoon granulated sugar

2 bird's eye chile peppers, thinly sliced

Roots of 1 bunch cilantro, sliced like chives

FOR SERVING:

2 limes, quartered

Crushed peanuts (optional)

Make the pork ribs: Preheat the oven to 250°F (120°C). With your fingers and a paper towel, clean the ribs by taking the silverskin off the back. Rub the mustard into the ribs, then season heavily with the five-spice powder.

Place the ribs on a rack in a baking sheet and cook in the oven 3 hours, until they are fork-tender but not falling off the bone. Heavily wrap in plastic wrap, then wrap in a dish towel and rest, 1 hour.

Make the cucumber salad: In a bowl, season the cucumber with the lime juice, vinegar, salt, and sugar. Add the chile peppers and cilantro roots; let marinate at least 1 hour in the fridge.

Unwrap the ribs and place on a clean baking sheet. Turn the oven to broil. Spoon the XO sauce over the entire rack of ribs and place under the broiler. Keep your eye on them. Once the ribs start getting sticky, after 1 minute, remove them from the broiler and add another coating of XO sauce. Return to the broiler and cook until crispy. Place on a cutting board.

To serve: Slice the ribs and put on your favorite plate. Add the limes and cucumber salad. Add some crushed peanuts, if desired. Help yourself.

Lamb Dandan Noodles

SERVES: 6
PREP TIME: 3 DAYS

**FOR THE FERMENTED
MUSTARD GREENS:**

1 bunch mustard greens, cut
into 2-inch (5 cm) pieces

2 tablespoons kosher salt

4 tablespoons (60 g) ground
turmeric

FOR THE DANDAN BROTH:

3 pounds (1.4 kg) pork bones

3 pounds (1.4 kg) lamb bones

4 onions, quartered (unpeeled)

2 carrots, peeled and cut
lengthwise

1 bulb fennel, quartered

2 jalapeño peppers, halved
(keep seeds in)

Canola oil

1 knob ginger, peeled and sliced

1 bunch parsley

3 bay leaves

1 bunch cilantro

2 tablespoons coriander seeds

2 tablespoons star anise

3 tablespoons black peppercorns

1 cinnamon stick

2 tablespoons allspice

5 cloves garlic, peeled

Kosher salt, if needed

Ingredients continue

Minced spicy lamb, fermented mustard greens, crushed peanuts, fermented chili paste, and spicy broth combined for a classic dish at Parts & Labour. I haven't had it in months, and I'm literally trying to figure out how to get some delivered to my desk while I'm writing this. Parts & Labour is closed right now, and I'm fucking starving.

The inspiration for this dish happened on a rainy night in Vancouver, which has amazing Asian restaurants. I was with some friends, and we were eating the best dumplings and noodles I'd ever had. The dandan was so spicy, and the funky mustard greens, the spicy oil, and the noodles were so incredibly good. I immediately wondered how I could make it at Parts & Labour. Make it spicier? Use lamb? I really hope you make this dish.

—

Make the fermented mustard greens: Place the mustard greens in a colander over a bowl and toss with 1½ tablespoons of the salt. Massage with your hands and let the water release. You want the greens to look withered. Give them a squeeze and really work them.

Bring 2 quarts (2 L) water to a boil. Add the remaining 2½ tablespoons salt and the turmeric. Stir to dissolve, then let cool completely.

Give the salted greens a quick rinse and use a salad spinner to dry them as much as you can. Place the mustard greens in a container with a lid. Pour the turmeric brine over them. Let sit 48 hours at room temperature, then refrigerate 24 hours.

Make the dandan broth: Preheat the oven to 400°F (205°C). Roast the pork and lamb bones until deep golden brown, 45 minutes.

Place the onions, carrots, fennel, and jalapeños on a baking sheet. Add a drizzle of oil and toss to evenly coat the vegetables. Place in the oven and roast alongside the bones until caramelized. Stir every 15 minutes so they char evenly, until golden brown, about 1 hour.

Place the bones and vegetables in a large stockpot and cover with cold water. Bring to a boil and skim the scum; turn the heat down to low and add the ginger, parsley, bay leaves, cilantro, coriander seeds, star anise, peppercorns, cinnamon stick, allspice, and garlic; simmer 4 hours.

Using a fine chinois, strain the stock into another pot. Bring to a boil and reduce by half, about 10 minutes. Season with salt, if necessary.

Recipe continues

4 cups (500 g) all-purpose flour, plus more for dusting

1 teaspoon baking soda

About 1 cup (240 ml) room-temperature water

FOR THE DANDAN MEAT:

½ cup (120 ml) canola oil

2 tablespoons minced fresh ginger

2 tablespoons peeled and minced garlic

2 tablespoons minced red chiles

½ cup (55 g) diced Spanish onion

2½ pounds (1.2 kg) ground lamb leg or shoulder

1½ tablespoons tomato paste

2 tablespoons Chinese five-spice powder

¼ cup (60 ml) creamy peanut butter

¼ cup (60 ml) hoisin sauce

2 tablespoons malt vinegar

Kosher salt

FOR SERVING:

Crushed peanuts, chopped cilantro, sliced cucumber, bird's eye chile peppers or sambal

Make the dandan noodles: Using a fork, combine the flour and baking soda in a bowl until thoroughly mixed.

Slowly add the water and knead the dough with your hands until it starts to come together. Place the dough on a work surface and knead until homogenous and slightly tacky.

Wrap the dough in plastic wrap and refrigerate at least 40 minutes.

Let the dough come back to room temperature, about 30 minutes.

Cut the dough into quarters and roll out each quarter into a thin sheet about ¼ inch (6 mm) thick. Cut each sheet into a square, roll into a tube, then slice into thin strips, running the knife across the rolled tube of dough. Toss the strips in flour so they don't stick, then gently dust them off and divide into 6 equal piles.

Make the dandan meat: In a large heavy-bottomed pot set over medium heat, heat half the oil. Add the ginger, garlic, red chiles, and onion (making a mirepoix); cook until golden and caramelized, 5 to 7 minutes.

Set a large cast-iron pan over high heat. Add the remaining oil, or just enough oil to cover the bottom of the pan. Place some of the lamb in the pan and sear it. Don't disturb the lamb until browned and caramelized, then flip it like a pancake, using a metal spatula. It will break apart, but that's okay. Sear the opposite side. Once you sear both sides, add to the pot with the mirepoix. Repeat with the rest of the lamb.

Add the tomato paste to the large pot of mirepoix and ground lamb. Cook 3 minutes, then add the five-spice powder and stir to incorporate.

Add 1 quart (960 ml) dandan broth and cook over medium heat about 10 minutes. Add the peanut butter, hoisin sauce, and vinegar. Stir and turn the heat down to low; leave until needed.

Put it all together: Reheat the remaining broth. Bring a pot of salted water to a boil. Place a portion of the noodles in the water 1 minute, then remove and place in a bowl. Scoop some dandan meat on top, then ladle some soup broth down the side of the bowl and fill only halfway up the noodles. Add crushed peanuts, fermented mustard greens, chopped cilantro, sliced cucumber, and some sliced bird's eye chile peppers or sambal, if you want it spicy.

Buffalo Sweetbread Sliders

—

SERVES: 4

PREP TIME: 4 HOURS

—

FOR THE PARKER HOUSE ROLLS:

¼ cup (60 ml) warm water

2 teaspoons active dry yeast

¼ cup (50 g) granulated sugar, plus a few pinches

1 cup (240 ml) room-temperature milk

½ cup (1 stick/115 g) unsalted butter, melted

3 whole eggs

1 tablespoon kosher salt

4 cups (500 g) all-purpose flour, plus more for dusting

1 egg yolk

2 teaspoons Maldon salt

FOR THE PICKLED RED ONION:

1 red onion, peeled and sliced into thin rounds

Juice of 1 lemon

2 tablespoons white vinegar

Sugar

Kosher salt

Ingredients continue

I love everything about this dish. I love buffalo wings and I love sweetbreads, so why not deep-fry beautifully poached sweetbreads and coat them in buttery hot sauce on a fresh Parker House roll? Once again, this is a dish that really shows how we cooked whatever we wanted at Parts & Labour. This dish is eight years old. Wow . . .

—

Make the Parker House rolls: In the bowl of a stand mixer fitted with the dough hook attachment, combine the water, yeast, and a few pinches sugar. Let the mixture stand until foamy, about 10 minutes.

Add the remaining sugar, the milk, half the melted butter, the whole eggs, and the kosher salt to the foamy yeast and mix on low until combined. Increase the speed to medium. Slowly incorporate the flour into the mixture and knead until a soft, sticky dough forms, about 5 minutes.

Turn the dough out onto a flour-dusted work surface. Knead the dough into a smooth, soft ball, using more flour as needed.

Grease a large bowl with some of the melted butter. Place the dough in the bowl and brush the surface with melted butter. Cover with plastic wrap and let sit until the dough has doubled in size, about 2 hours.

Place the dough on a flour-dusted surface. Using a rolling pin, roll the dough into a 10 by 12-inch (25 by 30.5 cm) rectangle.

Cut the dough into 12 equal rectangles. Brush melted butter over half of each rectangle, widthwise. Grease a 9-inch (23 cm) square baking pan with melted butter.

Fold the dough rectangles in half. Place them in the greased pan 3 across and 4 down. Cover tightly with greased plastic wrap and let rise in a warm place 30 minutes.

Meanwhile, preheat the oven to 350°F (175°C).

In a small bowl, mix the egg yolk with 1 tablespoon water. Brush the egg wash over the dough and sprinkle with Maldon salt. Bake in the oven until golden brown, about 45 minutes. Let stand 5 minutes before removing from baking pan.

Recipe continues

1 cup (135 g) crumbled blue
cheese

½ cup (120 ml) sour cream

1 cup (240 ml) mayonnaise

Zest and juice of 1 lemon

1 tablespoon white vinegar

10 cracks fresh black pepper

1 teaspoon kosher salt

FOR THE SWEETBREADS:

1 cup (240 ml) Frank's RedHot
original sauce

½ cup (1 stick/115 g) unsalted
butter

1 tablespoon garlic powder

1 tablespoon cayenne powder

Sea salt

2 pounds (910 g) sweetbreads

2 cups (250 g) all-purpose flour

3 eggs, whisked

1 cup (80 g) panko bread
crumbs

4 cups (960 ml) canola oil

FOR SERVING:

1 head iceberg lettuce, sliced
into chiffonade

Make the pickled red onion: Place the red onion in a bowl. Add the lemon juice, vinegar, 3 pinches sugar, and 2 pinches salt; mix with your fingers. Let sit at room temperature until the onions turn bright pink, about 30 minutes, then place in the fridge until needed.

Make the blue cheese dressing: Add all the ingredients to a food processor and blitz 1 minute.

Make the sweetbreads: In a cold pan, pour the hot sauce and add the butter, garlic powder, and cayenne. Warm gently, whisking; do not boil. Keep warm until needed.

Bring a pot of salted water to a boil. Rinse the sweetbreads under cold water 15 minutes. Blanch the sweetbreads 5 minutes, then transfer to an ice bath 10 minutes until chilled. Slice the sweetbreads into 2-ounce (55 g) portions, and peel off any extra membrane.

Set up a breading station: Place the flour in a bowl, the eggs in another bowl, and the panko bread crumbs in another bowl. First dust the sweetbreads in the flour, then dip in the eggs, then coat in the panko, and place on a rack set on a baking sheet.

In a deep pot, heat the canola oil. Once the oil has reached a temperature of 325°F (165°C), carefully fry the sweetbreads until golden and crisp on the outside and warm in the center, 3 to 5 minutes. Place on a baking sheet.

Gently toss the sweetbreads with the hot sauce.

Put it all together: Slice the Parker House rolls in half; in a nonstick pan, toast them. Place a little blue cheese dressing on the bottom buns. Top with lettuce, the buffalo sweetbreads, a few pickled red onions, and some more blue cheese dressing to ooze all over everything. Close with the top of the rolls.

Pigtail Tacos

SERVES: 6
PREP TIME: 4 DAYS

FOR THE PIGTAILS:

3 large pigtails

4 onions, peeled and halved

1 carrot, peeled and halved lengthwise

2 Roma tomatoes, halved

2 stalks celery, halved

FOR THE BURNT CABBAGE "KIMCHI":

2 heads red cabbage, halved, cored, and leaves separated

½ cup (120 ml) ketchup

½ cup (120 ml) hoisin sauce

½ cup (120 ml) soy sauce

½ cup (120 ml) fish sauce

½ cup (120 ml) malt vinegar

1 cup (240 ml) sambal

1 cup (240 ml) yuzu juice

½ cup (120 ml) lime juice (about 6 limes)

1 cup (240 ml) canola oil

1 cup (240 ml) rice wine vinegar

5 cloves garlic, peeled

1 knob ginger, peeled

1 bunch cilantro, chopped

¼ cup (24 g) Korean chile powder

Ingredients continue

How do you make pigtails desirable in Toronto? Put them in a taco that's made out of a scallion pancake, that's how! The pigtail is a perfect ratio of meat, fat, and skin. Now, what if you took that tail, braised it, picked all those tiny bones out of it, pressed it, fried it, and served it on a fluffy made-to-order scallion pancake with a burnt red cabbage kimchi? You've got yourself a home run. I like the cabbage more than the tail, but together it's an unstoppable force that sold well. This was on the menu for a few months, and we took it off the menu because we wanted to, not because we needed to. I love when that happens—choosing to take a beloved dish off the menu always feels great. It feels like you won a little league baseball tournament. It's over, but it's on your own terms.

—

Make the pigtails: Place the pigtails in a pot with cold water; bring to a boil. Once it boils, drain and rinse the pigtails quickly under running hot water. Return the pigtails to the pot and add cold water; bring to a boil again. Skim any scum that rises, then add the onions, carrot, tomatoes, and celery; simmer 2½ hours. Turn off the heat and let steep 30 minutes.

Remove the pigtails and let cool until you can handle them. Then, using a sharp boning or paring knife, cut out the bones (it should be easy now that they are braised) and, with gloved hands, pick them out. Cut the tails into bite-size pieces and mix up so that there's meat, fat, and skin all intertwined, and place in a parchment-lined loaf pan. Cut a piece of cardboard that can fit over top of the loaf pan to act as a lid and wrap in plastic, then press and refrigerate overnight.

Make the burnt cabbage "kimchi": Preheat the broiler; place a baking sheet on the highest oven rack to get hot. Pull out the baking sheet and place one layer of cabbage leaves on it (do not add any oil or seasoning). Return to the oven and broil until the leaves are burnt. You don't want to turn them to dust, but you do want them to actually burn. When the cabbage is burnt on one side, flip the leaves and burn the other side. Repeat with all the cabbage leaves, then place in a bowl.

In a large stainless-steel bowl, combine the ketchup, hoisin sauce, soy sauce, fish sauce, malt vinegar, sambal, yuzu, lime juice, oil, and rice wine vinegar; stir with a whisk. In a blender, blitz the garlic, ginger, cilantro, and Korean chile powder until it's pulp, then add to the bowl. If the sauce is too thick, add some water. This is a really intense sauce so it should be loose, like a nice watery mega-punch flavor bomb to the face. Add the cabbage to the sauce and stir to coat; wrap the bowl with plastic wrap and refrigerate 24 hours.

Recipe continues

1 cup (125 g) all-purpose flour

2 eggs

2 cups (480 ml) whole milk

1 cup (240 ml) heavy cream

1 bunch green onions

1 tablespoon canola oil

Kosher salt

Cooking spray

FOR SERVING:

1 bunch radishes, sliced

Jalapeño chiles, sliced

1 bunch cilantro, chopped

Make the scallion pancakes: Place the flour, eggs, milk, cream, green onions, oil, and 1 teaspoon salt in a high-power blender and blend on high for 1½ minutes. The mixture will turn completely green. Pour into a pitcher, wrap with plastic wrap, and refrigerate until needed.

Coat a nonstick pan with cooking spray and set over medium heat, then using a 2-ounce (60 ml) ladle, pour 1 pancake in the pan. Wait until the sides bubble and you can lift the edge of the pancake, then flip. Continue to make the scallion pancakes until the batter is finished; you should have about 20 pancakes.

Put it all together: Slice the pigtails into ½-inch- (12 mm) thick portions. In a nonstick pan, place 2 portions of the pigtails and cook over medium-high heat until golden brown, 3 to 4 minutes. Flip with a spatula. (It will get pretty spitty with the skin and fat, so be careful.) Place the crispy fried pigtails on a paper towel–lined plate.

Prepare a plate of the pancakes, a plate of the fried pigtails, a bowl of the burnt cabbage, and bowls of sliced radishes, sliced jalapeños, and chopped cilantro.

Let your guests make their own crispy, fatty tacos wrapped in warm little fluffy pancakes.

The Cauliflower

—

SERVES: 4

PREP TIME: 6 HOURS PLUS
AN OVERNIGHT BRINE

—

FOR THE CAULIFLOWER:

1 large cauliflower, quartered

10% brine (page 182)

FOR THE CELERIAC BROTH:

4 celery roots

4 yellow onions (unpeeled)

Kosher salt

FOR THE ARTICHOKE CHIPS:

6 Jerusalem artichokes

1 tablespoon white vinegar

3 cups (720 ml) canola oil

Kosher salt

FOR THE SALSA VERDE:

1 cup (240 ml) olive oil

½ bunch parsley

½ bunch cilantro

½ bunch basil

½ bunch tarragon

½ bunch mint

1 jalapeño, chopped

1 shallot, peeled and chopped

1 clove garlic, peeled and
chopped

Zest and juice of 1 lemon

Kosher salt and freshly ground
black pepper

FOR SERVING:

¼ cup (60 g) ricotta cheese

There have always been a lot of chefs in the culinary world serving whole roasted cauliflower. I feel brining the cauliflower is very important to the integrity of the end product. If you season just the outside, nothing on the inside will have flavor. Brining vegetables is something as old as time, but very few people do it now. The celeriac broth is so easy to make and, once again, reaps big rewards on this dish. The deep, slow-roasted celeriac flavor steeped for a few hours is amazing on its own, but with fried cauliflower; bright salsa verde; creamy, acidic ricotta; and crunchy Jerusalem artichoke chips, it may be one of the best vegetarian dishes I've ever made.

—

Brine the cauliflower (see page 182) for 24 hours. Let air-dry on a baking sheet 2 to 3 hours.

Make the celeriac broth: Preheat the oven to 300°F (150°C). Place the celery roots and onions on a baking sheet and roast in the oven 4 hours.

Place the caramelized celery roots and onions in a large pot and cover with water; bring to a boil and simmer 1 hour. Turn off the heat and let steep 30 minutes, then strain through a fine chinois into another pot. Season with salt to taste.

Make the cauliflower: Preheat the oven to 450°F (230°C). Roast the cauliflower 10 minutes, until the outside is soft but the core is slightly firm.

Make the artichoke chips: Using a mandoline, shave the Jerusalem artichokes into a bowl of 3 cups (720 ml) cold water and the vinegar. Place the Jerusalem artichokes into a paper towel–lined bowl.

In a large pot, pour the canola oil. When the temperature of the oil reaches 350°F (175°C), fry the Jerusalem artichokes until golden brown. (Stand back from the pot to avoid spitting oil.) Place in another paper towel–lined bowl and season with salt. Now, fry the whole cauliflower in the same pot until golden brown.

Make the salsa verde: In a bowl, combine all the ingredients and mix. Consistency should be mulchy.

To serve, pour 6 tablespoons (90 ml) broth in the bottom of each bowl. Place a piece of cauliflower in the middle of each bowl, spoon some ricotta on top, then spoon on some salsa verde. Top with a handful of the crispy Jerusalem artichoke chips.

TERRINE BOARD: WHO REALLY CARES ABOUT CHARCUTERIE ANYMORE AND HERE'S A LITTLE DITTY ABOUT KUNGFU

We served a terrine board at Parts & Labour for three years. We offered half and full portions. Kungfu was the man behind our charcuterie program. It got out of control sometimes. Some weeks we would make so many different terrines, pâtés, and sausages that we would literally put like eight slices of whatever we were making on the board. Neglecting food cost at every corner. Kungfu called them his projects. Instead of doing regular prep for his station, he often would be working away on one of his projects—elbow-deep in sausage farce or stuffing a bladder for nduja.

I love that guy so much. I first met him at La Palette, where he was a young and eager culinary school kid learning to cook. We clicked immediately. We were both small-town boys who loved to party—like really party. We were inseparable for years. It was awesome. At P&L we were able to go wild with food, making whatever we wanted. It was the best—until it wasn't. I'll say this: If you have ever shared time with Kungfu at a show, a bar, or rolling around on a beach in some part of the world, you know that you are really living in the moment. He is truly one of a kind. I am lucky to call him a brother after all these years.

When he and I parted ways at Parts & Labour, it wasn't the best time in our relationship. We were both drunk every day and slowly started resenting each other. We worked for a lot of years together. I was always his chef, but we were equal in his eyes. I agree with that now but definitely did not then. The egos of young chefs are pretty blinding and deafening at times. We were both good cooks; but that could not keep us together.

My friend Giuseppe and I were having an espresso at Parts & Labour one day. He was talking about how he needed a chef for a new diner he was opening and asked if I knew anyone for the job. Right at that moment Kungfu walked through the dining room. I laughed and asked, "Hey, Kungfu, you want to be a chef at a new diner?" He said, "Yup!" And that was it.

Kungfu and I parted ways. He opened an amazing diner called Wallace & Co. Kungfu absolutely killed it. The food was amazing and the setting was so perfect. He really makes some of my favorite food. I love his corned beef hash. After about a year, the restaurant suffered a bad fire and Kungfu was out of a job. So he finally got back to what he loved: making charcuterie—hot dogs, specifically, and that's how his awesome business Kungfu Dawg was birthed.

I'm so proud of him and proud to be his friend. Charcuterie was his baby and I could not have opened Parts & Labour without him. Here's a picture of our terrine board that I made for the photo shoot for the cookbook, but Kungfu wasn't around (he was out of the country) to give me any of his recipes—so there are no recipes. A picture is worth a thousand pâté en croûtes.

His name is Stephen Edward Payne.

Goose, Squab, Quail,
and Foie Gras Pithivier

Headcheese

Wild Boar
Rillettes

Country Pâté

Oxtail and
Snail Terrine

Vietnamese Steak Tartare

SERVES: 4
PREP TIME: 1 HOUR

FOR THE VIETNAMESE STEAK TARTARE:

1 pound (455 g) beef tenderloin

1 carrot, peeled and diced

1 daikon, peeled and diced

½ cup (120 ml) white vinegar

½ cup (100 g) granulated sugar

Kosher salt

Zest and juice of 2 limes

¼ cup (60 ml) fish sauce

½ cup (120 ml) olive oil

1 cup (140 g) smoked mussels

1 cup (240 ml) mayonnaise

4 egg yolks

½ cup (70 g) crushed peanuts

1 bunch cilantro, stems thinly sliced

4 green onions (white parts only), thinly sliced

1 bunch Thai basil leaves, quartered

1 bunch mint, leaves halved, then quartered

3 tablespoons Korean chile powder, for garnish

6 bird's eye chile peppers, thinly sliced, for garnish

2 jalapeños, sliced, for garnish

Ingredients continue

I had a dish in Montreal that blew my mind: a raw beef salad with pretty much everything that goes on a banh mi: pickled daikon, carrot, crushed peanuts . . . I straight up stole the flavors, added the smoked mussel aïoli, and changed the plating. This is what raw beef should taste like. And this shrimp toast is based on the best shrimp toast I've ever had, at Rang's sister's house in Phan Rang, a few hours south of Ho Chi Minh City in Vietnam. It was so simple and delicious. The best thing about shrimp cakes and toasts is that they are just as good hot as they are cold. That's where the seasoning for the whole dish comes into play—the fish sauce, the rendered pork fat, the cilantro. I'm proud of this dish, and I'm proud that I'm taking influences from around the world. It's important to make things your own and acknowledge the food that has inspired you.

—

Make the Vietnamese steak tartare: Place the beef in the freezer 30 minutes so it's easier to slice and dice. Slice the beef into ½-inch (12 mm) rounds, then dice. Place in a bowl, cover with plastic wrap, and push down so there's no air in the bowl; refrigerate until needed.

Make a quick pickle: Place the carrot and daikon in a bowl. In a pot, pour 1 cup (240 ml) water, the vinegar, sugar, and 3 tablespoons salt; bring to a boil and pour over the daikon and carrot. Cover and refrigerate to cool.

In a bowl, place the lime zest and juice, the fish sauce, and oil; stir.

Drain the mussels and place in a food processor; add the mayonnaise and blitz until fully incorporated. Using a spatula, scoop the mixture into a squeeze bottle and place in the refrigerator until needed.

Remove the beef from the refrigerator and coat with the lime–fish sauce oil (make sure to stir before using). You don't want to make the beef wet—you just want an even coating, 2 to 3 tablespoons. Add a pinch or two of salt.

Spoon a quarter of the beef onto a plate. Make an indent in the meat with your spoon. Place 1 egg yolk in the hole. Squeeze about 1 tablespoon of the smoked mussel mayo next to the egg. Use a slotted spoon to remove the pickled carrot and daikon from their liquid; drain on a paper towel, then spoon some around the beef. Add some crushed peanuts on top and sprinkle the meat with the cilantro stems, green onion whites, basil, and mint. Make sure to leave the yolk uncovered. Finally, dust the yolk with some of the chile powder, and garnish with chiles and jalapeños. Repeat for the other plates.

Recipe continues

3 bird's eye chile peppers

4 cloves garlic, peeled

1 thumb-size (1-inch/2.5 cm) knob ginger, peeled

8 sprinkles fish sauce

3 ounces (85 g) lard

1 pound (455 g) peeled and deveined black tiger shrimp

6 thick slices white bread

1 cup (150 g) white sesame seeds, untoasted

Canola oil

Make the shrimp toast: In a food processor, place the bird's eye chile peppers, garlic, ginger, fish sauce, and lard and blitz until smooth. Add the shrimp and blitz some more until smooth. Add just a little ice-cold water if the mixture is too tacky.

Spread the shrimp paste evenly over the bread, ¼ inch (6 mm) thick, then cut and trim the bread into fingers.

Pour the sesame seeds on a plate. Dip the bread in the sesame seeds and make sure it is completely covered.

In a large nonstick pan set over medium-high heat, pour 3 tablespoons oil. Cook the shrimp toast until the seeds are toasted and the shrimp cooks through: Once you get the perfect golden sesame-seed crust, flip from side to side every 30 seconds, 3 or 4 times. Place on a paper towel–lined plate. In between each toast, wipe the pan clean with a paper towel and add fresh oil. You should be able to cook 2 to 3 toasts at once, but don't crowd the pan.

Put the shrimp toast fingers on the side of your plate and dig into that tartare.

Nashville Hot Chicken

—

SERVES: 4

PREP TIME: 3 HOURS PLUS
AN OVERNIGHT BRINE

—

FOR THE CHICKEN:

2 (3 to 4-pound/1.4 to 1.8 kg) chickens

10% brine (page 182)

Canola oil

Kosher salt

FOR THE FLOUR MIXTURE:

4 cups (500 g) all-purpose flour

¼ cup (25 g) onion powder

3 tablespoons garlic powder

¼ cup (25 g) cayenne

3 tablespoons paprika

2 tablespoons ground fennel seed

Kosher salt and freshly ground black pepper

FOR THE HOT OIL:

2 cups (240 ml) canola oil

10 Scotch bonnet chile peppers

10 bird's eye chile peppers

5 jalapeños

2 cups (4 sticks/455 g) unsalted butter

½ cup (50 g) cayenne

½ cup (50 g) smoked paprika

Ingredients continue

I love Nashville style hot chicken in the same way I love buffalo wings. It's one of those dishes that can be served in any restaurant in some version or another. A lot of Canadians don't understand that hot chicken is actually spicy. This is the dish I miss the most from Parts & Labour. I'd eat one thigh and one drum, Nashville style, with a scoop of mashed potatoes, some collard greens, cream corn, pickles, and Texas toast. This shit is fire.

—

With a good pair of kitchen scissors, cut out the spine of the chicken; discard. On a cutting board, use a large knife to cut off the legs, then slice in between the thigh and the drumstick, separating them. Flip the bird over so the breasts are on the cutting board and cut the bird in half, then cut each breast in half. Repeat with the second chicken. A whole chicken should give you 10 pieces: 4 breasts, 2 thighs, 2 drumsticks, and 2 wings. Place the 20 pieces of chicken in a pot; brine (see page 182) for 24 hours.

Make the flour mixture: In a large bowl, place the flour, onion powder, garlic powder, cayenne, paprika, fennel seed, salt, and pepper; stir with a whisk.

Remove the chicken from the brine and pat dry with paper towels, then add to the flour mixture; refrigerate 2 hours.

In a large Dutch oven, pour the canola oil halfway up the pot. Place a candy thermometer in the oil and heat until the temperature reaches 325°F (165°C).

Separate the wings, breasts, thighs, and drumsticks. Before adding to the canola oil, dust the chicken one last time in the flour mixture to make sure there are no wet spots.

Add the wings to the canola oil; fry 9 minutes and place on a rack and season with salt. Let the oil temperature come back to 325°F (165°C).

Add the drumsticks to the oil; fry 10 minutes and place on a rack and season with salt. Let the oil temperature come back to 325°F (165°C).

Add the thighs to the oil; fry 13 minutes; place on a rack and season with salt. Let the oil temperature come back to 325°F (165°C).

Add the breasts to the oil; fry 16 minutes; place on a rack and season with salt.

Recipe continues

1 cup (100 g) cayenne

½ cup (50 g) smoked paprika

Thick slices white bread

Bread and butter pickles

Make the hot oil: In a pot over high heat, heat the canola oil and the Scotch bonnet, bird's eye, and jalapeño peppers until a candy thermometer reaches 350°F (175°C); turn off the heat and let steep 30 minutes. Pour into a blender, filling only halfway to avoid overfilling, and blend. Pass through a fine chinois into a medium pot. Heat again, then add the butter, cayenne, and paprika; stir with a whisk.

Make the finishing powder: In a bowl, combine the cayenne and paprika.

Spoon the hot, spicy oil over the chicken on the resting rack. Sprinkle the finishing powder over the hot chicken. Serve with Texas toast and pickles.

The P&L Pork Belly Pancake
with Maple Trotter Sauce

—
SERVES: 6
PREP TIME: 4 HOURS
—

FOR THE PANCAKES:

1 cup (128 g) all-purpose flour

1½ tablespoons sugar

1 teaspoon salt

1½ teaspoon baking powder

1½ teaspoon baking soda

1 tablespoon unsalted butter, melted

2 eggs, separated

1 cup (240 ml) buttermilk

Cooking spray

FOR THE MAPLE TROTTER SAUCE:

4 pig's feet

1 onion, peeled and sliced

2 cloves garlic

6 sprigs thyme

1 tablespoon black peppercorns

1 bay leaf

2 cups (480 ml) Madeira wine

4½ cups (1 L) veal stock

2 cups (480 ml) maple syrup

Kosher salt

FOR SERVING:

½-pound (225 g) pork belly, cut into 4 pieces

4 eggs

Unsalted butter, for frying (optional)

This dish has four of my favorite things: pig's feet, pancakes, pork belly, and maple syrup. It's a dish that has been on the menu since day one, standing the test of time. Fergus Henderson invented this sauce. So thank you, Fergus!

—

Make the pancakes: Sift the flour through a sieve into a large bowl. No one wants lumpy pancakes, so this will help prevent that. Sift the sugar, salt, baking powder, and baking soda into the bowl and stir all the ingredients together. Set aside.

Melt the butter over medium-low heat. Do not burn the butter. Set aside to cool in the pan. Crack the eggs and separate the yolks and the whites, save both. Whisk the egg whites until fluffy. Add the buttermilk to the egg whites.

In a separate bowl, stir the yolks until blended. Stir in the sugar, then add the cooled, melted butter to the egg yolk mixture. Whisk the yolk mixture into the egg white mixture until fully incorporated. Slowly whisk the flour mixture into the wet mixture so that no clumps form. Whisk to fluffy consistency and refrigerate 10 minutes.

Make the maple trotter sauce: Place the pig's feet in a pot with 4½ cups (1 L) cold water. Bring to a boil. Discard water and rinse feet to get rid of all the scum. Now, once again, place feet in pot and add 4½ cups (1 L) cold water and bring to boil. Turn down to a simmer. Add onion, garlic, thyme, peppercorns, and bay leaf. Simmer 3 hours or until meat is tender. Skim the scum. If no scum rises that's great. You've just made stock.

Take feet out of the stock and place on a clean surface. Gently pick out all of the little pig feet bones. There are plenty, so be careful and thorough. Next, dice the pig feet meat and place in a pot with the wine, 2 cups (480 ml) veal stock, and 1 cup (240 ml) maple syrup, and simmer 30 minutes. Taste for salt.

Generously coat a large skillet over medium-high heat with cooking spray. Spoon a cookie-size portion of batter into the pan. Don't press on them or fuck with them at all. Let them sit there and get tasty. When you see bubbles forming in the middle and a nice browning on the sides it's time to flip them (only do this once).

In a small skillet, fry the pork belly; drain on a paper towel. Fry 4 eggs sunny side up in the pork fat, or you can wipe the pan and put in a small bit of butter.

Put a pancake or two in the middle of a plate, a piece of pork belly on top, and then a beautiful sunny side up egg on top of that. Surround with a moat of maple trotter sauce. Share with loved ones.

The Super Festival County Doughnut (Not a Beaver Tail)

MAKES: 1 BIG-DOG DOUGHNUT

PREP TIME: 1 HOUR

FOR THE DOUGHNUT:

2 cups (480 ml) whole milk

1 cup (240 ml) warm water

3 tablespoons instant yeast

2 tablespoons plus 1 cup (200 g) granulated sugar

4 eggs

1 tablespoon vanilla extract

1 cup (240 ml) canola oil, plus more for the bowl

2 teaspoons kosher salt

8½ cups (1 kg) all-purpose flour

FOR THE CINNAMON SUGAR:

1 cup (200 g) granulated sugar

¼ cup (24 g) ground cinnamon

I hate making desserts, so here's the greatest giant doughnut recipe you've ever seen. At Parts & Labour I was stupid enough to call it a beaver tail, which I later found out was trademarked, so we got a cease-and-desist order stating that we were going to get sued if we continued to sell beaver tails. So, I was like, fuck that; this is just deep-fried dough, so let's call it the Super Festival County Doughnut.

—

Make the doughnut: Combine the milk and water in a pot over medium-low heat until a candy thermometer reaches above body temperature. Add the yeast and 2 tablespoons sugar and let sit in a warm place until foamy and fragrant.

In the bowl of a stand mixer with the whisk attached, mix the 4 eggs, 1 cup (200 g) sugar, and the vanilla extract on medium-high speed until fluffy and pale in color.

Reduce the speed to medium and slowly pour in the oil until the mixture is thoroughly combined.

Reduce the speed to low and slowly add the activated yeast mixture and the salt.

Turn off the mixer and replace the whisk attachment with the dough hook. Slowly add the flour at medium speed until the dough is completely combined and slightly tacky.

Place the dough in an oiled bowl and allow to proof in a warm area for at least 1 hour.

Fill a large Dutch oven halfway with oil and heat over medium heat until it reaches 325°F (165°C). Fry dough until golden brown. It will puff up like a pita. Flip it back and forth. Put it on a resting rack.

Make the cinnamon sugar: In a large bowl, combine the sugar and the cinnamon.

Cover your doughnut with the cinnamon sugar. Fill your boots.

The P&L Burger

SERVES: 6
PREP TIME: 1 HOUR

FOR THE BACON-ONION JAM:

1 pound (455 g) slab bacon, sliced into lardons

2 cups (4 sticks/455 g) unsalted butter

4 pounds (500 g) onions, sliced

1 cup (240 ml) red wine vinegar

¼ cup (50 g) sugar

FOR THE BURGER:

3 pounds (1.4 kg) fresh ground brisket

Kosher salt and freshly ground black pepper

1 cup (145 g) diced kosher dill pickles

1 cup (240 ml) Hellmann's mayonnaise

1 pound (455 g) Monterey Jack cheese, sliced

Unsalted butter

6 sesame-seed milk buns

Shredded iceberg lettuce

I am known for cheeseburgers, and I hate it. We always had a cheeseburger on the menus at Parts & Labour and Oddfellows. Everyone loves cheeseburgers. But then I did a cheeseburger competition TV show in Toronto called *Burger Wars*. It was my first time on television, and I won. After it aired, Parts & Labour turned into a burger shop. People were driving from places like Cornwall and Niagara Falls, like four to seven hours, to try the "best burger in Toronto." We used to change the burger every two months, but then we were stuck with the burger I made on the show. It's still on the menu now, eight years later.

It's so wild how something like that can change a whole restaurant. I didn't go to cooking school and bust my ass at two of the best French restaurants in Canada to cook cheeseburgers. We literally had to change the kitchen to keep up. We raised the price of the burger, trying to deflect people into trying some other dishes. It really blew all our minds. I feel grateful for every person who walks into any of my restaurants—there are so many great choices out there. For someone to commit and say they want my food has always been a humbling feeling.

But let's get back to hating this cheeseburger. We even opened a cheeseburger shop for a few years to try to divert business away from Parts & Labour. It failed because we did it for the wrong reasons. I didn't care about cheeseburgers and neither did any of the partners. Opening a restaurant for any reason aside from the fact that you truly love it will result in failure. Life is very short and you only have a small window to do what's right and make life great.

Even while I'm writing this, the burger brings up mixed emotions: It made so many people happy, but there was something that ate away at my soul every time it left the kitchen. Holy fucking shit, that's a lot to take in. Make this burger as much as you want, but please don't talk to me about cheeseburgers ever again.

—

Make the bacon-onion jam: In a large heavy-bottomed pot set over medium heat, render the bacon. Add the butter and onions. Cook over low heat, stirring occasionally, 1½ hours. Cooking the onions this slowly will let them caramelize naturally in their sugars.

Add the vinegar and sugar to the pot and cook 15 minutes, then remove from the heat. Let cool and place in container and store in the refrigerator. (When you make the P&L Burgers, you can warm some of this jam in a pan.)

Make the burger: Place cast-iron skillet over medium heat 5 minutes before cooking the patties.

Roll 6-ounce (170 g) burger balls from the brisket and pat them into flat, thick patties, about 1 inch (2.5 cm) thick. Season the patties with salt and pepper.

Recipe continues

In a bowl, combine the pickles and mayonnaise; set aside.

Place three patties in the skillet (with no oil). The fat will render and you will have a juicier burger from the natural fat inside the patty. Cook 4 minutes on one side, then flip.

Top each patty with the jam and then put 2 slices of cheese per patty on top. Pour 2 tablespoons water into the skillet, covering it immediately so the burgers can steam. Remove the lid after 45 seconds. The cheese should be fully melted.

Butter the buns and place them facedown in another skillet over medium-high heat so they get nice and toasty.

Spoon the pickle mayo on the bottom buns, then add a good pile of the lettuce. Add the cheesy beef patties, cover with more of the pickle mayo, then add bun tops.

Just eat the fucking burger.

World peace

THE FINAL WORD

Don't forget the struggle.

Don't forget the streets.

Don't forget your roots.

Don't sell out.

Ray "Raybeez" Barbieri
RIP, never forget

November 27, 1961–September 11, 1997

ACKNOWLEDGMENTS

Family: Patricia, Macarthur, Mom, Dad, Nanny and Grampy Poirier, Nanny Tucker and Grampy Matheson, Sarah, Steve, Adam, Cameron, Cail, Iris, Frank, Racheal, Scarlet, Jack, JF, Bill, Carol, Rebecca, Jeff, Reece, Evan, Deanna, Rob, Judy

My team: Matthew Langille, Myke Bulley, Rebecca Humboldt, Andrew Turner, Chris Taylor

Friends: Marika, Scrap, Wade and Lauren, Snelgrove, Jaye, Mikey, Scoeb, Rachel, Porter, JFT crew, Ryan, Jason, Mark, Thatcher, Cro-Mags, Matt, Kate Coleman and Sawyer, Bert and Ruth Marlowe, and Bonnie, Chris, Jen and Ollie, Scott V., GQ and Nicole, Max, Rocco, and Giacomo, Nicky P. and his girlfriend, David and Ranit, Lev, Liat, Basilio and Teo, Neil Young, Rob, Audrey, Reecey, Derek, CC, Felix, Dave and Fred, Marco and Vanya, Emma, Ryan, Danny and Chuck and the Night Cheetah, Helen Hollyman, Elana, Farideh, John Martin, Chris Grosso, Lauren Cinnamon, Earth Crisis, Shane, Tamyka, Eddy, Suroosh and Zanab, Lee Boy, Kate and the Boys, Adam Perry Lang, Benny, Josh R., Dave G., Steph G., Matty D. and Erin, Frank Falcinelli, Frank Castronovo, Minor Threat, Nacho and Thomas, Riad, Clint and his tribe, Nate Hindle, Amy and Ruby; Laura, Rich, and Harvey Hope, Michelle, Sal Zoo and Jesse, Susanne, Steven and Henry, Katie, Macon and Ruby, Bad Brains, Morgy and Cookie, Scotty Cigs, Estevan Oriol, Matt McCormick, Leeroy, Cali, Alexis, Zach, Alex, Spanto, Born x Raised friend group, North Shore Crew and Kauai Boys, Barca, Kai, Leaf, Kala, Kyle, Hugh, Rico, Danny, Lyndie, Axel, Bruce, Irons Family, Fletcher Family, The Band, RVCA crew, Pat, Brian, Oblow, Zach, Brophy, Bobby, Luke, Jay, Barlow, Bruce, Stu, Michael, Ian, Zack, Curren, Jeff, Mendes Boys,

Breath Bruh Brian, Stefan, Sage, Marshall, Austin, Kona, Jon Roth and Tash, KOOPZ, JR, Scarr, Jazz, Quailty, Billy and Hometown BBQ, Freaky Franz, Bert Krak, Christian, Rene, Nadine, James, Cath, Kumin, Maya, Nickolai, Bo, Duncan, Joe Beddia, Shlomo, Teddy, Curtis D., Tort, Sound Guy, Harvey, Patrick, Jon, Lisi, Garrett, Brendan Schuab, Drama, Sean and Death Rites, Angelo, the Needle Street X, Jon and Vinny, Chris and Sarah, Evan Funke, Morty, Tony, Colin, Baxter, Biscuit Slut, Sean G. and Ko, Gman, Dave C., Carlo, Danny B., Eddie H., Ray, Morna and Bernie, Jacob Dockendorf and Bobby MacIsaac of Atlantic Shellfish

Book crew: Garrett McGrath, Quentin Bacon, Pat O'Rourke, Deb Wood, John Gall, Danielle Youngsmith, food stylist Michelle Rabin, Alex Goodall

Restaurant shout-outs: Le Sélect Bistro—Vickie and JJ, Chris Taylor Wright, Stephan, Master Rang, Barb, Ciara, Siva, Ratnam. La Palette—Shamez, Maria, Artedio "Super Model Death Walk," Missy, Castle, Lenny, Shelly and Joe. Oddfellows—Kei, Brian, Bloody, Streets, Ordenda, Jesse B. Harris, Allison, Millman, Grandma, Captain Buzzkill, Mattitude, and everyone that I shared a key bump with in the Winnebago, I'm happy I don't remember you. Parts & Labour—Richard, Jesse, Brian and Kei, Matthew Demille, Brenty, Kungfu, Goodall, Geoff Martin, Hamilton, Robbie T., Matt T., Kanamotes, Chantel, Kumar

I could write this forever. I'm very thankful for all the amazing people in and around my life, you all inspire me daily with positivity. Everyone I've forgot, anyone I've ever cooked with, and everyone that has this book in their hands, I LOVE YOU.

INDEX

297